ONE-POT HEALTHY MEALS

Delicious Recipes from
Pan to Plate in 30 Minutes or Less

CHRISTINA SHOEMAKER
Creator of The Whole Cook

FAIR WINDS

Quarto.com

First Published in 2020 by Fair Winds Press, an imprint of The Quarto Group,
100 Cummings Center, Suite 265-D, Beverly, MA 01915, USA.
T (978) 282-9590 F (978) 283-2742

28 27 26 25 24 1 2 3 4 5

ISBN: 978-0-7603-9605-6

The content in this book was previously published as *Clean Paleo One-Pot Meals: 100 Delicious Recipes from Pan to Plate in 30 Minutes or Less* by Christina Shoemaker (Fair Winds Press, 2020).

Design: Samantha J. Bednarek
Cover Image: Christina Shoemaker
Page Layout: Samantha J. Bednarek
Photography: Christina Shoemaker and Meredith Brown on pages 5 and 10.

Printed in China

contents

introduction

I am a food lover. If you know me at all, you know this to be true. I wake up thinking about what to eat, and by the time I've finished any meal, I'm planning my next.

My grandmother used to say I was like a bird because when I was small, I'd stand at her feet in her tiny white kitchen with my mouth open, ready for her to drop something in. Not much has changed.

While I was always someone who loved to eat, I was not always confident in the kitchen. And I most certainly wasn't making healthy food choices. In my twenties, I relied heavily on prepackaged microwave dinners and fast-food chain restaurants to keep me fed. If it was fried (and came with fries), I wanted it. I also had a six-pack-a-day soft drink habit and consumed copious amounts of vending machine snacks for breakfast at work each morning.

It wasn't until I became a mother that I developed any interest in cooking. All of a sudden, I was responsible for what food went into my children's growing bodies. Talk about pressure! I may not have known much about nutrition, but I most certainly knew that fast-food burgers and fries were not what they needed.

So, I started asking questions, reading books, and searching the Internet to better understand what the heck this whole clean eating thing was about. I was hooked right away. The idea of focusing on whole-food ingredients and limiting processed foods made complete sense to me. It just clicked.

I became an enthusiastic home cook, preparing every meal for my family and experimenting with ingredients I hadn't worked with before. My confidence in the kitchen skyrocketed. I could do this! I could prepare wholesome dishes for my children and husband—and they actually liked them!

As my confidence grew, I started documenting our meals each day on my Instagram account. I'd snap quick photos on my phone, unconvinced that anyone would be interested. Boy, was I wrong! There was tons of interest! I loved connecting with other people on there who were also pursuing a healthier lifestyle.

It wasn't long before the idea of a blog popped up. What if I had a place to share my recipes instead of just the pretty pictures of them? (Okay, those photos were not pretty. They were grainy and dark. I should be clear about that.)

On that blog, *The Whole Cook*, I learned a lot about creating yummy recipes the whole family would enjoy. My own personal family of food critics thoroughly tested each one. And trust me, nobody is more skeptical of whatever meal is placed in front of her than my five-year-old daughter.

Since 2016, I've shared hundreds of delicious recipes as The Whole Cook, and my top performers are always the 30-minute meals. Whether it's in a skillet, baking dish, single pot on the stove, or on a sheet pan in the oven, these recipes are the dishes that get made, shared, and raved about. And now with this cookbook, I'm bringing you 100 of my very favorites. Hopefully, they'll become your favorites too.

My blog readers have made it clear what they're looking for and why.

people want to feed their families healthy food but feel overwhelmed by it.

When dinnertime arrives, they are out of time, uninspired, and ready to just be done with the day. All those big Pinterest plans have flown out the window. Who has time (or the desire!) to stand in a hot kitchen chopping, simmering, and then cleaning for two hours? No, ma'am. Count me out on all of that.

I want to do as little as possible in the kitchen and still create a nutritious meal for my family.

fast food doesn't have to be junk food.

There's just something immensely satisfying about tossing all the ingredients on a sheet pan and letting everything roast. A few minutes after popping the pan in the oven, that incredible aroma fills the kitchen. Does June Cleaver live here? Nope. But she could.

You feel like Ina Garten when you pull that finished pan from the oven, but alas, you didn't have to hike the Alps to gather your ingredients or spend hours doing prep. Does it taste like you did? Indeed, it does.

This cookbook isn't for the Ina Gartens of the world. This cookbook is for those of us who want to feel like her in only 30 minutes. Those people are my people.

healthy food doesn't have to be complicated or weird.

The problem with so many good-for-you dishes (no matter how much time they take to make) is that often they come off as a little strange. A little *too* good for you.

Sure, you could swap a dehydrated kale wrap for a tortilla, but do you really want to?

Yes, you could prepare a pitcher of raw spinach, cucumber, and ginger juice to sip on every day, but again, do you want to?

I'm not alone when I say there is no way on God's green earth my family would be on board with any of those healthy solutions.

we want to eat healthy without it tasting like a punishment.

A healthy chili should still look and taste like the chili of your childhood. A stir-fry should taste *better* than takeout and not like a poor substitute.

My recipes are popular because they taste good while still being good for you.

The dishes you'll find in *Clean Paleo One-Pot Meals* are simple but flavorful; impressive but fast and easy; and perfect for the busy parent feeding a family or the individual who wants to meal prep for the week.

I'm so excited to share these recipes with you and can't wait for you to give them a try. I look forward to hearing how you incorporate them into your mealtime routine!

recipe icon key

Each recipe has one or more of the following icons for quick reference.

ICON	TERMINOLOGY	DEFINITION
	**Dairy-free**	These recipes do not contain the milk from mammals (such as cows or goats) or any food products made from milk.
	**Egg-free**	These recipes do not contain any eggs or any egg by-products.
	**Vegetarian**	These recipes do not contain meat but may include ingredients made from animal by-products such as eggs, honey, or ghee.
	**Vegan**	These recipes do not contain meat or any ingredients made from animal by-products such as eggs, honey, or ghee. Some recipes with this icon have a vegan-friendly alternative included.
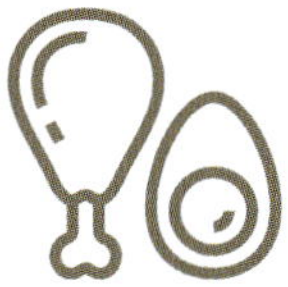	**Keto**	These recipes include ingredients that are lower in carbohydrates and are perfect for a low-carb diet.

1

the basics

When I first set out to adopt a healthier way of eating, I was afraid it would be too limiting. I feared a future of boiled chicken, egg whites, and kale. I can't even begin to stress how much I dislike the idea of eating huge quantities of kale. Gag. It would be my nightmare come to life.

And eating that kind of bland food just isn't sustainable. I can't do it. I love food too much! I want it to taste good while also making my body feel its very best. Is that too much to ask?

No, friend, it's not.

My other worry as I began transforming my family's eating habits was that it was going to take too much time. Now, I happen to love being in the kitchen. This should come as no surprise, since I voluntarily create recipes for my blog every single week. But when it's dinnertime, I'm ready to get out of that kitchen. Sound familiar? I want to be lying horizontal with a book or playing a card game with my sassy five-year-old and hilarious nine-year-old. I do not want to be creating a giant mess and then cleaning up said giant mess while everyone else sits around relaxing. Hard pass.

So, let's make eating healthy approachable.

the clean paleo approach

What's the big picture?

I don't like to label what we eat as good or bad. I believe that kind of thinking is a slippery slope and can create an unhealthy relationship with food. But does that mean all food is created equal? Well, no. Not even close.

Some foods are simply more nutritious for us than others. They fuel us, giving us more energy, and even help us get better rest at night.

And some foods don't have much nutritional value at all. They can fill our tummies for a little bit but make us feel sluggish and tired. We function better and we feel better when we limit those types of things. Recognizing that is the first step in making real, positive changes.

How you change your eating habits is completely up to you. Your answer may very well be different from mine, and that's okay! My goal is to arm you with quick, healthy recipes so it's easy for you and your family to eat well.

So What the Heck Is Paleo?

I have great news for you. There's no need to grab that bow and arrow or till the field for seed planting. Cleaning up your diet doesn't have to be complicated.

Let's dig in to what Clean Paleo means.

Unfortunately, you may very well come across some conflicting information out there about which foods are considered Paleo. It's totally okay. I like to keep things very simple.

If you're sticking to the most straightforward definition (which I am), Paleo means noshing on a diet of quality whole foods. We're talking about the unprocessed eats here. Let's focus on nutrient-dense, vitamin-packed foods wherever possible. They should make our bodies stronger, our brains sharper, and our sleep more restful.

It seems like common sense, right? Well *of course* we want to eat what makes us healthier. But, as you know, this is actually a drastically different approach than our current Western diet, which is heavily processed, loaded with preservatives, and includes an astonishingly high number of ingredients that are possibly linked to various illnesses. Many folks see a correlation between the foods of today and the dramatic rise in chronic illness and obesity. We also tend to have more stress, more inflammation, and get less sleep. Now, genetics, environment, and lifestyle play a big role too, but nobody disputes that the food we put into our bodies is a factor worthy of examination. It's why there's such a growing interest in the clean eating movement.

i'm in! so, what can i eat?

Oh, so much good food!

But before we go further, let me make this disclaimer: THIS IS YOUR DIET. It's not my diet, your friend's diet, or the diet of that woman in the gym wearing the neon-green full-body spandex. You should make the choices that make the most sense for you. Period. I'm going to explain what a Paleo-inspired diet can look like, but take what you want from it.

If you're wanting to hear from someone who is rigid in their commitment to kale, I am not for you. Looking for someone who doesn't fill their home with Christmas cookies in December? I am not your gal. Pass me all the cookies. But someone who carefully chooses healthy foods 85 percent of the time and believes in balance? Oh look, that's me!

Disclaimer over. Back to your question.

A Paleo-inspired diet includes lots of lean meat, poultry, seafood, vegetables, fruit, nuts, seeds, and healthy fats. Phew. Doesn't sound terrible, right? Plus, throw in plenty of dried herbs and spices for flavor. (I assure you I don't eat bland food. Ever.) There are even great sweeteners to play around with and a wide assortment of Paleo flours for baking. See? All good things.

I promise there is no shortage of good-for-you and totally delicious grub that fits perfectly in the Paleo-inspired diet.

Meat, Poultry, and Seafood

Select wild-caught seafood wherever possible. Let's pick on salmon for a minute to understand why. Farmed salmon is fed a processed feed that's higher in fat in order to yield very big fish. This dramatically changes the nutritional content of the salmon you eat. Not only does farmed salmon have more calories, fat, and sodium than wild salmon, but various studies indicate that farmed salmon also contain more *toxins* and *contaminants* than wild salmon. Toxins are scary. So, go wild, friends.

When purchasing meat, try to stick to grass-fed and organic wherever possible. It's not always an option, especially when eating out or if you find your grocery store offerings to be particularly limiting, but when available, it's the better way to go. The same goes for poultry.

Eggs

I can think of 100,000 ways to prepare eggs. They're so incredibly versatile! They're also easy to make and affordable. But which eggs to buy? Organic is always your best bet. When it comes to how the birds are cared for, pay special attention to pasture raised or free range. The chickens producing these eggs have some room to roam and forage for bugs. I like to think this leads to happier chickens and perhaps better eggs. Score!

Vegetables & Fruits

I eat my weight in veggies every day, and if you think that's an exaggeration . . . well, you're obviously right. But I do really love my veggies. That's what I'm getting at.

Organic veggies and fruits are ideal because we can avoid those unwelcome pesticides. Buying fresh produce in season and staying stocked up with frozen or canned options (always unsweetened and in natural juices) will help save money.

Fats

Want to add a bit of crunch to a salad or stir-fry? Need a quick snack? Nuts and seeds are the perfect solution. Honestly, there isn't much in this world that I enjoy more than a spoonful (or four) of almond butter.

Other amazing fats to include in your diet are extra-virgin olive oil, avocado oil, sesame oil, walnut oil, macadamia nut oil, coconut oil, and ghee. That's not an exhaustive list, but those are the main ones. When you see "cooking fat of choice" listed as an ingredient in a recipe here, those are the ones I'm referring to. Take your pick!

Flours

If you enjoy baked goods or want to thicken a sauce or soup, there are some fantastic flours I encourage you to try. My favorites are almond flour, arrowroot flour, coconut flour, tapioca flour, and Paleo flour (which is basically a premade blend of some of the others mentioned). These options are delicious, but not exactly the same as highly processed white flour. They're gluten free, brown more quickly, can have a slightly different texture, and are minimally processed. You can really create some fun dishes with these once you get used to how to work with them. (Don't worry—I'll show you!)

Sweeteners

Raw honey, maple syrup, coconut sugar, Medjool dates or date syrup (if made of 100 percent dates), and fruit juices are phenomenal sweeteners you can use in beverages, sauces, baked goods, and more. While you don't want to go crazy and guzzle a lot of the stuff, you can happily incorporate them into your healthy lifestyle. Just keep in mind that natural sugar is still sugar, so be conscious of your intake.

Vinegar

Vinegar is highly underrated as a way to maximize flavor. I personally love it to transform soups, sauces, and salad dressings. White, red wine, white wine, balsamic, apple cider, and rice vinegars are all fair game. Remember that a little goes a long way because they pack a punch!

what to avoid?

We've covered all the delicious foods we can enjoy on a Paleo-inspired diet, but let's discuss what you may want to consider avoiding and why.

Refined and Added Sugars

Sugar occurs naturally in any food that contains carbohydrates, so nobody is suggesting that we completely eliminate it in all forms. Instead, how about we focus on *added* sugar? When you start reading food labels, you'll be surprised by how many packages list sugar (or sucrose, high-fructose corn syrup, dextrose, or malt syrup) as an ingredient. That's added sugar. That's different than the naturally occurring sugar found in foods.

So why do companies add it to so much? The obvious answer is to sweeten the product, but sometimes, it's simply to change the texture or extend the shelf life. We consume so much of this added sugar without even realizing it (because we're definitely not paying attention) that we end up with way more in our diet than is good for us. And, we're oblivious to it!

So, pay attention. Step out of the dark, friend. Read your labels. Skip or limit the added sugar.

Grains

This is a tough one for lots of people. A standard Paleo diet does not include wheat, barley, rice, corn, oats, or quinoa. But don't sweat it! You can re-create lots of the traditionally gluten-filled fare with gluten-free Paleo ingredients!

Legumes

Beans, peanuts, lentils, and soy are typically avoided because of the high amount of lectins and phytic acid they contain, which may be linked to leaky gut (doesn't that sound pleasant?). A ban on soy includes edamame, tofu, and tempeh, and once you start reading labels, you're going to see that soy is added to almost *everything*. But wait! There are some yummy legumes you can still munch on. Green beans, snow peas, and sugar snap peas are all good to go!

That said, there is a second perspective that feels consuming legumes in small doses may be worthwhile. They're low in fat and high in fiber, protein, and iron. Soaking and cooking the legumes may deactivate most of the lectins and drastically decrease the amount of phytic acid. The choice is yours.

Vegetable Oils

These oils are highly processed because the types of oils in this category come from plants that really make you work for their oil. Examples include soybean oil, corn oil, rice bran oil, sunflower oil, safflower oil, peanut oil, cottonseed oil, and canola oil. (Imagine trying to make oil from a kernel of corn or a sunflower seed. It would take some work! Whereas olives, avocado, and coconut can yield plenty of oil with minimal processing because they contain plenty of fat.) And hey, there are an abundance of awesome oils available to us that just plain work better!

Highly Processed Foods

Processed foods generally include many of the things listed here to avoid, especially grains (hello, white flour!), added sugars, and hydrogenated vegetable oils. They're also designed to make you want to eat more, so it's easy to overindulge.

Keep things simple. Choose quality whole foods with minimal processing. If an ingredient label is full of items you can't pronounce, it's likely something that would fall in the highly processed food category.

and now the confusing foods

The good and the bad are fairly cut-and-dried, but there are a few foods that are often debated in the Paleo community. Those conversations can create a ton of confusion. Do you eat it or not? Maybe. That choice is yours.

Do a little personal experimentation, friend. I suggest sticking to a strictly Paleo diet for 30 days. See how you feel. Then, if there are a few things you're wanting to try again, do that. How does your body respond? Do your research and decide for yourself.

Potatoes

The biggest concerns regarding white potatoes are a) they're starchy, b) they have a high glycemic index, c) it's very easy to overindulge in them, and d) they're all too often used in highly processed and completely unhealthy ways. I concede all of these points. However, I recognize all the complex carbohydrates, antioxidants, dietary fiber, potassium, and other nutrients that potatoes give us. They can actually help our bodies fight inflammation! So, does my family eat potatoes? Yes, we do. But I am sure to prepare them in healthy ways and in moderation.

Since the general consensus is that sweet potatoes are the healthiest option in the potato family, I've included them in several recipes in this cookbook. If you prefer to swap it for another potato, go for it. If you want to skip the sweet potatoes completely and use other veggies that requires a similar cooking time, such as green beans, carrots, or butternut squash, go for it.

Decide on the Big Potato Issue for yourself. Know that whatever you choose is great!

Dairy

Oh dairy, you complicated beast.

The vast majority of Paleo or clean eating advocates say dairy is a no. The milk sugar *lactose* is not well tolerated in many people, the milk protein *casein* can harm your gut lining, and there's some talk that milk may increase your risk of certain cancers.

The widely accepted exception to the no-dairy rule is ghee—glorious, delicious ghee. You'll see it in many of my recipes, both here and on my blog. What is it? Oh, friend, if you're new to ghee I'm going to change your life. Ghee has actually been around forever, originating in ancient Indian cooking. It is butter that's slowly simmered until it separates into liquid fat and milk solids. When those milk solids are removed, it's nearly lactose free and casein free! (It also makes it ideal for frying because there are no solids left to burn.) There's growing evidence that there are health benefits to eating ghee, which is wonderful news for this ghee lover. And my husband, who has a mighty powerful dairy allergy, can consume ghee with no issues! (To all of you with dairy allergies, I'm not saying to try it for yourself. Talk to your doctor. I'm just a woman with a blog and a kitchen.)

2

throw-together breakfast dishes

I never tire of breakfast food. How about you? In fact, I believe breakfast shouldn't be limited to that first meal of the day. I'll whip up a hash or frittata for lunch or dinner when the craving hits!

sheet-pan steak & eggs

Growing up, I remember my dad getting so excited for steak and eggs whenever we'd eat out. As an adult, I understand what all the fuss was about. It's typically not something you want to make at home because preparing a steak can be quite a lot of work. We usually want our breakfasts to be quick! This sheet-pan breakfast solves that dilemma for you. Enjoy steak, eggs, and crispy broccoli for a very satisfying and impressive start to your day!

PREP TIME 5 minutes
TOTAL TIME 30 minutes
MAKES 3 to 4 servings

12 ounces (340 g) broccoli florets

2 tablespoons (28 ml) extra-virgin olive oil

1 pound (455 g) top sirloin steak, cut into strips ½ inch (1 cm) thick and 3 to 4 inches (7.5 to 10 cm) long

¼ teaspoon garlic powder

¼ teaspoon salt, plus more to taste

¼ teaspoon black pepper

6 to 8 large eggs

1. Preheat the oven to 425°F (220°C, or gas mark 7).

2. Place the broccoli on a 12 x 17-inch (30 x 43 cm) baking sheet and drizzle with the oil. Toss until coated and then spread in a single layer. Bake for 15 minutes (see Tip).

3. Remove from the oven. Mix the steak with the broccoli and then spread out on the baking sheet. Season with garlic powder, salt, and black pepper. Move the florets and steak around to create six to eight spaces for your eggs. Crack an egg into each hole and sprinkle with salt.

4. Bake until the egg whites are set and the egg yolks are cooked to how you like them, another 7 to 10 minutes. (Watch those eggs as they cook!)

TIP

- I love my roasted broccoli extra crispy, but if you prefer it less crispy, just reduce that initial broccoli cooking time from 15 minutes down to 12 minutes.

chicken sausage frittata

This fully loaded frittata is inspired by my all-time favorite breakfast casserole by a similar name, but it cooks even faster. It's packed with flavor thanks to the salsa whisked into the eggs, and the chicken sausage, spinach, and riced sweet potato.

PREP TIME 10 minutes
TOTAL TIME 30 minutes
MAKES 8 slices

2 tablespoons (28 ml) extra-virgin olive oil or (28 g) ghee (For dairy-free dishes, use extra-virgin olive oil.)

½ white or yellow onion, diced into ½-inch (1 cm) pieces

1 cup (about 5 ounces, or 140 g) riced or shredded sweet potato (see Tip)

9 large eggs

½ cup (130 g) salsa

½ teaspoon salt

½ teaspoon black pepper

1 packed cup (about half a 5-ounce, or 140 g, package) baby spinach

2 fully cooked chicken sausages, sliced ¼-inch (6 mm) thick (see Tip)

1. Preheat the oven to 425°F (220°C, or gas mark 7).

2. Add the oil or ghee, onion, and sweet potato to a cast-iron skillet over medium-high heat. Sauté until the onion is softened and the potato has some browning, stirring frequently, 3 to 5 minutes.

3. Meanwhile, whisk together the eggs, salsa, salt, and black pepper in a large bowl. Set aside.

4. When the onion is done, turn off the stove. Spread the onion and potato mixture across the bottom of the skillet so it is evenly distributed. Layer the spinach leaves on top and then layer on your chicken sausage. Pour your egg mixture over everything.

5. Bake until the center is just set, 18 to 20 minutes. Check to make sure the center isn't very wiggly and then remove from the oven. Let it rest for a few minutes before serving.

TIP

- I use chicken sausage that's gluten and casein free and has no added nitrates. Use whatever brand you like or even swap it out for beef or turkey sausage!
- I use frozen riced sweet potato. The only ingredient is sweet potato. I don't even thaw it before sautéing! You can also shred or rice your own sweet potato at home if you prefer.

spicy sausage & egg skillet

Use your favorite precooked sausage to create a flavorful egg scramble that packs some heat! Amp up the intensity with extra hot sauce in the eggs and a hefty dose of sriracha before serving.

PREP TIME 5 minutes
TOTAL TIME 15 minutes
MAKES 4 servings

3 tablespoons (42 g) ghee, divided (see Tip)

1 cup (70 g) sliced mushrooms

2 precooked sausages, sliced ¼ inch (6 mm) thick

1 teaspoon minced garlic

8 large eggs

1½ teaspoons hot sauce (see Tip)

¾ teaspoon salt

¼ teaspoon chipotle chile powder

Sriracha sauce

1. Add 2 tablespoons (28 g) of the ghee, the mushrooms, and the sausage to a large skillet over medium-high heat. Sauté until the mushrooms are soft and the sausage has some browning, 3 to 4 minutes. Add the garlic. Stir and give it a quick sauté, about 1 minute, to achieve a golden color.

2. Meanwhile, whisk together the eggs, ¼ cup (60 ml) water, hot sauce, salt, and chile powder in a medium bowl. (The water helps make the eggs a little more fluffy since we're not using milk.)

3. Reduce the heat to medium-low. Add the remaining 1 tablespoon (14 g) ghee to the skillet. Pour the egg mixture over the mushroom mixture. The eggs will begin cooking right away. Use a spatula to fold the cooked outer edges of the eggs toward the center. Do this repeatedly until you don't have any more liquid in the pan.

4. Serve topped with a hearty drizzle of your favorite sriracha sauce.

TIP

- You can easily substitute a different cooking fat for ghee if you're completely dairy free or just prefer an alternative. I use ghee because it's my absolute favorite for eggs!
- Check out the ingredients in your hot sauce and sriracha sauce.

fried eggs with sweet potato rounds

Sometimes, you don't need anything more than eggs and potatoes. This whole dish cooks in less than 15 minutes. It's perfect for two!

PREP TIME 5 minutes
TOTAL TIME 25 minutes
MAKES 2 servings

1 medium sweet potato, cut into ¼-inch (6 mm)-thick rounds

½ teaspoon salt, plus more to taste

½ teaspoon paprika

2 tablespoons (28 g) coconut oil

1 tablespoon (15 g) ghee (see Tip)

2 to 4 large eggs

Black pepper, to taste

1. In a large bowl, toss your potato rounds in the salt and paprika so they're well seasoned.

2. Add the oil to a large nonstick skillet over medium-high heat. Once hot, add half of the potato rounds. You should hear a sizzle when you add them to the skillet. Cook for 2½ to 4 minutes until the side touching the skillet has some browning. Flip and cook for another 2½ to 4 minutes. Remove the rounds from the skillet and place on a paper towel–lined plate.

3. Repeat with the remaining potato rounds. If you're low on oil, add another ½ tablespoon before doing the second half. All the potato rounds should be on the plate when finished.

4. Reduce the heat to medium and wipe out the skillet.

5. Add the ghee to the cleaned skillet. Once melted, crack the eggs on one side of the skillet and sprinkle with salt and black pepper. Place the potato rounds beside the eggs. Cover the skillet and cook until the egg whites are set and the egg yolks are cooked to how you like them, about 3 minutes.

TIP

- You can easily substitute a different cooking fat for ghee if you're completely dairy free or just prefer an alternative. I use ghee because it's my absolute favorite for eggs!

turkey bacon baked egg cups

Eggs and bacon are the two most essential breakfast items of all the essential breakfast items. Am I right? I'm right. So, let's bake them together! If you're new to cooking with turkey bacon, you'll quickly discover that there are some fantastic brands and some less fantastic brands. I really recommend the thick, minimally processed turkey bacon you'll find in the natural foods section of your grocery store. It's so much more delicious, it's better for you, and it will better replicate that pork bacon we all grew up loving.

PREP TIME 5 minutes
TOTAL TIME 27 minutes
MAKES 12 egg cups

1½ to 2 tablespoons (23 to 28 ml) extra-virgin olive oil

12 slices turkey bacon, halved crosswise

12 large eggs

Salt and black pepper

1. Preheat the oven to 400°F (200°C, or gas mark 6). Grease a 12-cup muffin tin with oil, making sure you cover both the sides and the bottom of each cup. Wipe up any excess oil so you don't have oil pooling in the bottom of the cups.

2. Crisscross 2 bacon halves in the bottom of each cup to create an *X*.

3. Bake for 10 to 12 minutes. If the bacon you're using is thick (you did buy the better bacon, didn't you?), bake for 12 minutes. If you're using a fairly thin bacon (typically what's available in most supermarkets), 10 minutes will be fine. Your bacon will not be quite done.

4. Remove from the oven and carefully crack an egg on top of the bacon in each cup. Sprinkle with salt and black pepper.

5. Place back in the oven for 10 minutes or until the egg whites are set and the egg yolks are cooked to how you like them. Serve immediately!

taco skillet breakfast hash

Hash is my go-to breakfast solution because you can throw anything into the skillet with diced potatoes and *voilà*! You made a hash! This one is especially fun because we also have peppers, onions, taco-seasoned ground turkey or beef, and homemade pico de gallo. Those are a lot of big flavors to start your day off right! Make it really special by topping it off with black olives, fresh cilantro, guacamole, and/or avocado slices.

PREP TIME 10 minutes
TOTAL TIME 30 minutes
MAKES 2 to 4 servings

BREAKFAST HASH & EGGS

2 tablespoons (28 ml) extra-virgin olive oil or (28 g) coconut oil

2 medium sweet potatoes, cut into ½-inch (1 cm) cubes

½ red bell pepper, diced into ½-inch (1 cm) pieces

½ green bell pepper, diced into ½-inch (1 cm) pieces

¼ yellow or white onion, diced into ½-inch (1 cm) pieces

½ teaspoon salt, divided, plus more to taste

¼ teaspoon black pepper, plus more to taste

½ pound (225 g) ground turkey or beef

½ teaspoon chili powder

¼ teaspoon garlic powder

¼ teaspoon onion powder

¼ teaspoon dried oregano

⅛ teaspoon paprika

4 large eggs

PICO DE GALLO

1 medium tomato, diced into ½-inch (1 cm) or smaller pieces

½ large onion, diced into ½-inch (1 cm) or smaller pieces

Handful of cilantro, chopped

Fresh lime juice, to taste

Salt, to taste

¼ to ½ small jalapeño, seeded and diced (optional)

1. Make the Breakfast Hash & Eggs: Add the oil to a large skillet over medium-high heat. Once hot, add the potatoes, bell peppers, and onion. Sauté, stirring occasionally, until the potatoes have browned, about 5 minutes. Stir in ¼ teaspoon of the salt and the black pepper. Remove from the skillet and set aside.

2. Add the ground meat to the skillet and return to medium-high heat. Crumble the meat using your spatula and sauté until browned and cooked through, about 7 minutes. Stir in the chili powder, garlic powder, onion powder, oregano, remaining ¼ teaspoon salt, and paprika.

3. Meanwhile, make the Pico de Gallo: In a small bowl, combine the tomato, onion, cilantro, lime juice, and salt. Stir and set aside.

4. Add the cooked potato mixture back to the skillet with the ground meat, stirring to combine.

5. Use your spatula to create four holes in the hash. Crack one egg into each hole and sprinkle with salt and black pepper. Cover the skillet and reduce the heat to medium. Cook until the egg whites are set and the egg yolks are cooked to how you like them, 5 to 8 minutes.

6. Top everything with your homemade Pico de Gallo. Garnish as desired.

muffuletta egg scramble

All those flavors we associate with a classic muffuletta sandwich can now be enjoyed for breakfast in this tasty egg scramble. Roasted red peppers, salami, olives, and parsley . . . this is definitely not your typical breakfast fare!

PREP TIME 10 minutes
TOTAL TIME 20 minutes
MAKES 4 servings

¼ cup (45 g) chopped roasted red peppers, drained

¼ cup (35 g) chopped salami or pepperoni

2 tablespoons (18 g) sliced kalamata or black olives

2 tablespoons (13 g) chopped pimento-stuffed green olives

1 tablespoon (4 g) chopped fresh parsley

1 teaspoon red wine vinegar

½ teaspoon minced garlic

8 large eggs

1 tablespoon (6 g) Italian seasoning

½ teaspoon salt

½ teaspoon black pepper

2 tablespoons (28 g) ghee (see Tip)

1. In a small bowl, stir together the roasted red peppers, salami or pepperoni, olives, parsley, vinegar, and garlic. Set aside.

2. In a medium bowl, whisk together the eggs, ¼ cup (60 ml) water (this helps make them fluffy), Italian seasoning, salt, and black pepper.

3. Add the ghee to a large skillet over medium heat. Once hot, pour in the eggs and the olive mixture. Use a spatula to fold the cooked outer edges of the eggs toward the center. Do this repeatedly until you don't have any more liquid in the skillet.

TIP

- You can easily substitute a different cooking fat for ghee if you're completely dairy free or just prefer the alternative.

sheet-pan breakfast fries

Who says fries aren't appropriate breakfast food? Don't listen to them. We don't need that kind of negativity in our lives. These breakfast fries are fun with baked eggs, diced turkey bacon, and an easy sauce! You'll definitely need a fork for these tender and loaded fries!

PREP TIME 10 minutes
TOTAL TIME 30 minutes
MAKES 3 servings

BREAKFAST FRIES & EGGS

3 medium sweet potatoes, sliced into sticks ¼ to ½ inch (6 mm to 1 cm) wide

3 tablespoons (45 ml) extra-virgin olive oil

½ teaspoon garlic powder

½ teaspoon paprika

½ teaspoon salt, plus more to taste

¼ teaspoon chili powder

6 slices turkey bacon, diced

6 large eggs

Black pepper, to taste

COMEBACK SAUCE

½ cup (115 g) high-quality mayo

1 tablespoon (15 g) ketchup

1 teaspoon fresh lemon juice

½ teaspoon Tabasco sauce or similar Louisiana-style hot sauce

½ teaspoon paprika

½ teaspoon garlic powder

½ teaspoon ground mustard

½ teaspoon salt

1. Make the Breakfast Fries & Eggs: Preheat the oven to 425°F (220°C, or gas mark 7). Line a 12 x 17-inch (30 x 43 cm) baking sheet with parchment paper.

2. Toss the sweet potatoes with the oil, garlic powder, paprika, salt, and chili powder on the prepared baking sheet. Spread in an even layer.

3. Scatter the bacon on the baking sheet with the fries.

4. Bake for 12 minutes.

5. Remove from the oven and create six spaces for your eggs. (Position the fries so that they will prevent the egg whites from running.) Crack one egg into each space. Sprinkle with salt and black pepper. Bake until the egg whites are set and the egg yolks are cooked to how you like them, 6 to 10 minutes.

6. Meanwhile, make the Comeback Sauce: In a small bowl, stir together the mayo, ketchup, lemon juice, Tabasco sauce, paprika, garlic powder, mustard, and salt.

7. When the fries are done, drizzle the sauce on top. Now, break out the forks!

TIP

- Check the ingredients on your mayo, ketchup, and Louisiana-style hot sauce. There are some really tasty brands available that are made with simple ingredients and no sugar.
- Comeback Sauce is a mayonnaise-based dipping sauce that originated in Jackson, Mississippi, and is thought to have its origins from Greek immigrants who settled in that area in the 1930's.

one-pan country breakfast

When you order a country breakfast in a restaurant, you'll usually receive a plate of cheesy eggs, potatoes with bell peppers, and ham or bacon. My spin on it is better for you but still ridiculously tasty. We're keeping it low carb with butternut squash, and it's dairy free, of course.

PREP TIME 5 minutes
TOTAL TIME 15 minutes
MAKES 4 serving

2 tablespoons (28 ml) extra-virgin olive oil, divided

1 red bell pepper, diced into ½-inch (1 cm) pieces

½ white or yellow onion, diced into ½-inch (1 cm) pieces

1 cup (140 g) diced butternut squash, ¾ to 1 inch (2 to 2.5 cm) cubes (see Tip)

1 cup chopped cooked (140 g) turkey, (150 g) ham, or (140 g) chicken

8 large eggs

½ teaspoon salt

¼ teaspoon black pepper

1. Add 1 tablespoon (15 ml) of the olive oil to a large skillet over medium-high heat. Once hot, add the bell pepper and onion. Sauté, stirring occasionally, for 2 minutes. (They won't be quite finished yet.) Add the squash and cooked protein. Sauté everything until the squash is tender, the onion is softened, and the bell pepper has some browning, 3 to 5 minutes.

2. Meanwhile, in a medium bowl, whisk together the eggs, ¼ cup (60 ml) water, salt, and black pepper. Set aside.

3. Reduce the heat to medium or medium-low. Add the remaining 1 tablespoon (15 ml) oil to the skillet. Pour the eggs over the squash mixture. Use a spatula to fold the cooked outer edges of the eggs toward the center. Do this repeatedly until you don't have any more liquid in the pan.

TIP

- Cut the butternut squash into cubes ¾ to 1 inch (2 to 2.5 cm) big. Some grocery stores carry prechopped squash in this very size. It's a huge time-saver!
- This is a great recipe for using leftover Thanksgiving turkey, rotisserie chicken, or holiday ham. Deli meat works well here, too.

skillet egg & veggie scramble

Are you tired of boring eggs? Well, this scramble will change your mind! Salsa and sautéed veggies make these eggs next-level good. You'll never want to make plain scrambled eggs again.

PREP TIME 5 minutes
TOTAL TIME 15 minutes
MAKES 4 servings

2 tablespoons (28 g) ghee, divided

1 cup (71 g) chopped broccoli florets

½ white or yellow onion, diced into ½-inch (1 cm) pieces

8 large eggs

¼ cup (65 g) salsa

½ teaspoon salt

¼ teaspoon black pepper

1 packed cup (about half a 5-ounce, or 140 g, package) baby spinach

½ cup (90 g) halved grape tomatoes

1. Add 1 tablespoon (14 g) of the ghee to a large skillet over medium-high heat. Once hot, add the broccoli and onion. Sauté, stirring occasionally, until the onion is tender and you see some browning on the broccoli, 3 to 5 minutes.

2. Meanwhile, whisk together the eggs, salsa, salt, and black pepper in a bowl. Set aside.

3. When the onions and broccoli are done, reduce the heat to medium or medium-low. Add the remaining 1 tablespoon (14 g) ghee to the skillet. Pour in the egg mixture, spinach, and tomatoes. Use a spatula to fold the cooked outer edges of the eggs toward the center. Do this repeatedly until you don't have any more liquid in the skillet.

salsa chicken egg muffins

These savory muffins are perfect for meal prep or for when you want a healthy breakfast option for a crowd. Serve them with extra salsa or even guacamole. Or, keep them stocked in the fridge for a grab-and-go breakfast!

PREP TIME 10 minutes
TOTAL TIME 20 minutes
MAKES 12 muffins

1½ tablespoons (25 ml) extra-virgin olive oil

12 large eggs

½ cup (130 g) salsa

½ teaspoon salt

½ teaspoon black pepper

¼ cup (8 g) chopped fresh spinach

¾ cup (94 g) shredded cooked chicken (see Tip)

Fresh jalapeño slices (optional)

1. Preheat the oven to 350°F (180°C, or gas mark 4). Grease a 12-cup muffin tin with the oil. Don't skimp on this or your eggs will stick. Make sure you grease both the sides and the bottom of each muffin cup.

2. In a large bowl, whisk together the eggs with the salsa, salt, and black pepper.

3. Pour the egg mixture evenly into each cup, so they're about three-fourths of the way full (or a little more).

4. Divide the spinach among each cup and use a fork to push the spinach down a bit. Divide the chicken among the cups. Add a slice of jalapeño to the top of your muffins, if using. (I do this for half of my egg muffins so that I have six that are spicy and six that aren't.)

5. Bake until the eggs are puffed and just set, about 20 minutes. Remove from the oven and set aside to cool. The egg muffins will puff up a lot while baking but will settle down over the next 5 minutes as they cool. Once cooled, use a fork or small spatula to gently pull the egg muffins from the pan.

TIP

- Purchase a rotisserie chicken from your grocery store to save time.
- Try these optional additions: diced onion, diced bell pepper, or fresh cilantro.
- To reheat muffins, microwave each for around 15 seconds, adding more time, if necessary.
- To freeze, pop completely cooled muffins into a resealable plastic bag and place them in the freezer. When you're ready to reheat, wrap each muffin in a wet paper towel (to help hold in the moisture) and heat in the microwave for about 30 seconds, adding more time, if necessary.

skillet sausage sweet potato hash

This simple hash has plenty of flavor and comes together in 25 minutes!

PREP TIME 10 minutes
TOTAL TIME 25 minutes
MAKES 4 servings

- 2 tablespoons (28 ml) extra-virgin olive oil or cooking fat of choice
- 2 cups (266 g) diced sweet potatoes, ½-inch (1 cm) cubes
- ¼ white or yellow onion, diced into ½-inch (1 cm) pieces
- 1 teaspoon salt, divided, plus more to taste
- ¼ teaspoon paprika
- ½ pound (225 g) ground turkey or pork sausage
- ½ teaspoon chili powder
- ½ teaspoon dried oregano
- ¼ teaspoon garlic powder
- ¼ teaspoon black pepper, plus more to taste
- 4 large eggs

1. Add the oil to a large skillet over medium-high heat. Once hot, add the potatoes and onion. Sauté, stirring occasionally, until the potatoes have browned and the onion is tender, about 5 minutes. Stir in ½ teaspoon of the salt and the paprika. Remove from the skillet and set aside.

2. Crumble the ground meat into the skillet and return to medium-high heat. Sauté until browned and cooked through, about 7 minutes. Stir in the remaining ½ teaspoon salt, chili powder, oregano, garlic powder, and black pepper.

3. Add the potatoes and onions back to the skillet. Use your spatula to create four holes in the hash. Crack one egg into each hole and sprinkle with salt and pepper. Cover the skillet and reduce the heat to medium. Cook until the egg whites are set and the yolks are cooked to how you like them, 5 to 8 minutes.

3

sheet-pan & baking-dish dinners

There's just something so satisfying about tossing everything on a sheet pan (or in a baking dish) and letting it all roast until it's time to eat. It almost feels like cheating, doesn't it? Surely, dinner should be harder than this? But no, my friend. No need to complicate things. Let's keep it simple!

lemon-garlic mahi mahi with carrots

A quick and buttery lemon-garlic sauce transforms this fish into something truly spectacular. Pair with tender carrots (one of my favorite veggies to roast because of their natural sweetness), and you won't be disappointed!

PREP TIME 5 minutes
TOTAL TIME 30 minutes
MAKES 4 servings

1 pound (455 g) carrots, peeled and cut into sticks

4 tablespoons (56 g) ghee, melted, or (60 ml) extra-virgin olive oil, divided

¾ teaspoon salt, divided

4 mahi mahi fillets (see Tip) (6 to 8 ounces, or 170 to 225 g, each)

1½ tablespoons (25 ml) fresh lemon juice

1 tablespoon (10 g) minced garlic

1 tablespoon (4 g) chopped fresh parsley

1. Preheat the oven to 425°F (220°C, or gas mark 7).

2. Spread the carrots in one half of a 9 x 13-inch (23 x 33 cm) baking dish. Top with 2 tablespoons (28 g) of the ghee and ¼ teaspoon of the salt. Bake for 15 minutes.

3. Remove from the oven and reduce the temperature to 375°F (190°C, or gas mark 5).

4. Add the mahi mahi beside the carrots. Top the fish with the remaining 2 tablespoons (28 g) ghee, remaining ½ teaspoon salt, lemon juice, and garlic. Bake until the fish is opaque and flakes easily with a fork, 9 to 10 minutes.

5. To serve, divide the carrots among plates, along with a piece of fish. Sprinkle the fresh parsley over the mahi mahi.

TIP

- You can easily swap out the mahi mahi for another fish if you like. Tilapia or flounder would work well!

easy cashew chicken

Serve up this easy chicken dish on any busy weeknight! Chicken, cashews, broccoli, red bell pepper, and the tastiest 4-ingredient sauce ever—what's not to love? It has all the flavor you want in exceptional takeout, but it's better for you. Feel free to swap out the chicken for pork tenderloin, if that's what you have on hand.

PREP TIME 10 minutes
TOTAL TIME 25 minutes
MAKES 4 servings

4-INGREDIENT SAUCE

½ cup (120 ml) coconut aminos

1 tablespoon (15 ml) rice or apple cider vinegar

1 tablespoon (10 g) minced garlic

¼ to ½ teaspoon crushed red pepper flakes

CASHEW CHICKEN & VEGGIES

1½ pounds (680 g) boneless, skinless chicken breast, cut into 1-inch (2.5 cm) pieces

12 ounces (340 g) broccoli florets, large florets cut in half or thirds

1 red bell pepper, sliced into strips

Salt and black pepper to taste

2 tablespoons (28 ml) extra-virgin olive oil

¾ cup (105 g) roasted cashews, salted or unsalted

1. Preheat the oven to 425°F (220°C, or gas mark 7).

2. Make the 4-Ingredient Sauce: In a bowl, whisk together the coconut aminos, vinegar, garlic, and red pepper flakes (use more for spicier flavor!). Set aside.

3. Make the Cashew Chickenn & Veggies: Spread the chicken in a single layer on one side of a 12 x 17-inch (30 x 43 cm) baking sheet.

4. Add the broccoli in a single layer beside your chicken.

5. Spread the bell pepper in a single layer beside the broccoli.

6. Sprinkle salt and black pepper over everything. Drizzle the oil over the broccoli and bell pepper. Drizzle half the sauce over the chicken. (Save the other half for later.) Bake for 10 minutes.

7. Remove from the oven and separate the chicken if it's sticking together. Make room for the cashews and add directly to the pan. Bake for 5 additional minutes.

8. Remove from the oven and make sure your chicken is cooked through, completely opaque and juices run clear. Layer the broccoli, bell pepper, chicken, and cashews in bowls or on plates. Drizzle the remaining sauce on top just before serving.

TIP

- In most recipes, I mention using parchment paper on your baking sheet. I don't use any for this particular recipe, but you're welcome to if you'd like to further minimize cleanup.
- I love to serve this recipe over steamed cauliflower rice to create larger portion sizes and add an extra boost of veggies!

arroz con pollo

This fun and light twist on a classic Spanish chicken dish is so flavorful you are going to want to make it again and again. Juicy chicken thighs coated in a homemade adobo seasoning bake with veggie-packed cauliflower rice for a bold sheet-pan meal.

PREP TIME 8 minutes
TOTAL TIME 30 minutes + rest time
MAKES 4 servings

ADOBO SEASONING

1½ teaspoons salt

1 teaspoon paprika

½ teaspoon dried oregano

½ teaspoon black pepper

¼ teaspoon chili powder

¼ teaspoon ground cumin

¼ teaspoon onion powder

¼ teaspoon garlic powder

CHICKEN

1½ to 2 pounds (680 to 900 g) boneless, skinless chicken thighs

1 tablespoon (15 ml) extra-virgin olive oil

CAULIFLOWER RICE

3 cups (12 ounces, or 340 g) cauliflower rice

1 cup (180 g) halved grape tomatoes

½ green bell pepper, diced into ½-inch (1 cm) pieces

½ red bell pepper, diced into ½-inch (1 cm) pieces

½ white or yellow onion, diced into ½-inch (1 cm) pieces

1 tablespoon (15 ml) extra-virgin olive oil

Small handful of fresh parsley, chopped

1. Preheat the oven to 425°F (220°C, or gas mark 7).

2. Make the Adobo Seasoning: In a small bowl, combine the salt, paprika, oregano, black pepper, chili powder, cumin, onion powder, and garlic powder. Set aside.

3. Make the Chicken: Pat the chicken thighs dry. Rub the oil on the chicken, focusing most of it on the top. Press all but 1 teaspoon of the Adobo Seasoning onto the top of your chicken. Place the chicken on one side of a 12 x 17-inch (30 x 43 cm) sheet pan.

4. Make the Cauliflower Rice: Spread the cauliflower rice on the empty side of your sheet pan. Add the tomatoes, bell peppers, and onion to the cauliflower. Drizzle the oil over the veggies and sprinkle on another 1 teaspoon Adobo Seasoning.

5. Bake for 20 minutes. This cooks fairly quickly since we're using boneless thighs. To crisp the top of the chicken a bit, broil on high for 2 to 3 minutes after the baking time finishes.

6. Remove from the oven and cover the sheet pan with aluminum foil. Let the chicken rest for 10 minutes so that it's tender and completely cooked through to a minimum internal temperature of 165°F (74°C). Top the Cauliflower Rice with the parsley before serving.

barbecue chicken thighs with spicy broccoli

I love using chicken thighs rather than chicken breasts when possible because they are close to impossible to overcook and stay so juicy! You will appreciate how tender these are. Slather them with a surprisingly easy homemade and sugar-free barbecue sauce for the perfect entree paired with crispy broccoli.

PREP TIME 8 minutes
TOTAL TIME 30 minutes + rest time
MAKES 4 servings

CHICKEN THIGHS & SPICY BROCCOLI

1½ to 1¾ pounds (680 to 795 g) boneless, skinless chicken thighs

3 tablespoons (45 ml) extra-virgin olive oil, divided

½ teaspoon salt, plus more to taste

Black pepper, to taste

12 ounces (340 g) broccoli florets

¼ teaspoon garlic powder

¼ teaspoon crushed red pepper flakes

BARBECUE SAUCE

1 cup (240 g) ketchup

½ cup (120 ml) coconut aminos

2 teaspoons chili powder

1½ teaspoons ground mustard

1 teaspoon apple cider vinegar

1 teaspoon minced garlic

1 teaspoon salt

¼ teaspoon garlic powder

1. Make the Chicken Thighs with Spicy Broccoli: Preheat the oven to 425°F (220°C, or gas mark 7).

2. Pat the chicken thighs dry. Rub 1 tablespoon (15 ml) of the oil on the chicken, focusing most of it on the top. Place the chicken on one side of a 12 x 17-inch (30 x 43 cm) sheet pan. Sprinkle with salt and black pepper.

3. Spread the broccoli in an even layer beside the chicken. Drizzle with the remaining 2 tablespoons (28 ml) oil. Sprinkle with the ½ teaspoon salt, garlic powder, and red pepper flakes.

4. Bake for 10 minutes.

5. Meanwhile, make the Barbecue Sauce: In a medium bowl, combine the ketchup, coconut aminos, chili powder, mustard, vinegar, garlic, salt, and garlic powder. Divide between two bowls and set aside.

6. Remove the chicken and broccoli from the oven and brush the chicken with half of the sauce. Reserve the remaining sauce for later.

7. Bake for another 10 minutes. To crisp the top of the chicken a bit, broil for 2 to 3 minutes after the baking time finishes.

8. Remove from the oven. Brush the remaining half of the sauce on top of the chicken. Cover the sheet pan with aluminum foil. Let the chicken rest for 10 minutes so that it's tender and completely cooked through to a minimum internal temperature of 165°F (74°C).

sheet-pan sausage & veggies

This is the meal I turn to on those busy weeknights when I'm just barely holding on until bedtime. It just doesn't get much easier than this. Chop. Drizzle. Sprinkle. Bake. BOOM. Dinner is served.

PREP TIME 10 minutes
TOTAL TIME 30 minutes
MAKES 4 servings

1 pound (455 g) green beans, trimmed and halved

1 pound (455 g) Brussels sprouts, trimmed and halved

4 fully cooked chicken sausages, sliced ¼ inch (6 mm) thick

3 tablespoons (45 ml) extra-virgin olive oil

Salt and black pepper to taste

1 tablespoon (10 g) minced garlic

1. Preheat the oven to 425°F (220°C, or gas mark 7).

2. Spread the green beans, Brussels sprouts, and sausage on a 12 x 17-inch (30 x 43 cm) baking sheet in a single layer.

3. Drizzle the oil over everything and sprinkle with salt and black pepper. Stir everything together so the oil is evenly distributed and then spread in a single layer.

4. Bake for 15 minutes.

5. Remove from the oven and add the garlic. Bake until the vegetables are tender with some crispy edges, another 5 to 10 minutes.

TIP

- Any fully cooked sausage will work well here, so feel free to use your favorite brand or go with turkey or beef.
- Green beans or Brussels sprouts can be swapped out for another veggie with a similar cooking time. Carrot sticks or diced potatoes (if diced fairly small) would be delicious!

baked fish & root vegetables

Roasting root vegetables caramelizes the natural sugar in them to bring out their sweetness. Combine that with a flaky white fish, here we are using cod, and you have one incredible meal!

PREP TIME 10 minutes
TOTAL TIME 30 minutes
MAKES 4 servings

ROOT VEGETABLES

2 cups (244 g) peeled, sliced carrots, ¼-inch (6 mm)-thick slices

2 cups (266 g) diced sweet potatoes, ½-inch (1 cm) cubes

1 red onion, sliced into large chunks

¼ cup (60 ml) extra-virgin olive oil

1 teaspoon salt

½ teaspoon black pepper

FISH

1½ tablespoons (25 ml) fresh lemon juice

1 tablespoon (4 g) finely chopped fresh parsley

1 teaspoon extra-virgin olive oil

¼ teaspoon salt

¼ teaspoon garlic powder

4 cod fillets (6 ounces, or 170 g, each)

1. Make the Root Vegetables: Preheat the oven to 450°F (230°C, or gas mark 8). Line a 12 x 17-inch (30 x 43 cm) baking sheet with parchment paper.

2. Spread the carrots, sweet potatoes, and onion on the prepared baking sheet in a single layer.

3. Drizzle the oil over the veggies and sprinkle with the salt and black pepper. Stir it all together so everything is coated. Spread in a single layer and then bake for 10 minutes.

4. Meanwhile, make the Fish: Combine the lemon juice, parsley, oil, salt, and garlic powder in a small bowl. Set aside.

5. Remove the pan from the oven and reduce the temperature to 425°F (220°C, or gas mark 7). Use a spatula to stir the vegetables. Spread in an even layer and create four holes or spaces on the baking sheet for your fish. Add the cod to the pan. Drizzle your lemon juice mixture over the top of the cod.

6. Bake until the fish is opaque and flakes easily with a fork and the vegetables are tender, 10 to 15 minutes.

balsamic flank steak

This juicy flank steak swims in a delicious vinaigrette and cooks with broiled peppers, onion, and mushrooms. The secret to this perfect steak is in the incredible and simple marinade, broiling at high heat, letting it rest before serving, and thinly slicing the steak across the grain when it's time to serve. Garnish with fresh herbs for a gorgeous meal.

PREP TIME 10 minutes + marinating time
TOTAL TIME 22 minutes + rest time
MAKES 6 servings

5 tablespoons (75 ml) extra-virgin olive oil, divided

¼ cup (60 ml) balsamic vinegar

¼ cup (60 ml) coconut aminos

1 tablespoon (2 g) chopped fresh rosemary

1½ teaspoons salt

1 teaspoon black pepper

1 teaspoon garlic powder

½ teaspoon onion powder

½ teaspoon chili powder

1½ pounds (680 g) flank steak

8 ounces (225 g) cremini or baby bella mushrooms, sliced

3 bell peppers of any color, sliced into strips

1 red onion, sliced into strips

1. In a resealable plastic bag or bowl, combine 3 tablespoons (45 ml) of the oil, vinegar, coconut aminos, rosemary, salt, black pepper, garlic powder, onion powder, and chili powder. Add the flank steak, seal the bag, and toss to coat. Refrigerate for a minimum of 1 hour and up to 12 hours before cooking.

2. When ready to cook, move the oven rack to 5 to 6 inches (13 to 15 cm) from the broiler and set the broiler to high. Grease a 12 x 17-inch (30 x 43 cm) baking sheet with the remaining 2 tablespoons (28 ml) oil.

3. Place the steak on the prepared baking sheet, leaving any remaining marinade in the bag or bowl for now.

4. Spread the mushrooms, bell peppers, and onion around the steak in an even layer. Drizzle the remaining marinade over the vegetables.

5. Broil for 6 minutes.

6. Remove the pan from the oven and flip your flank steak. Broil for another 6 minutes for medium-rare.

7. Remove the pan from the oven. Cover with aluminum foil and let the steak rest for at least 10 minutes. This results in more tender meat.

8. Slice the meat thinly against the grain when ready to eat. Don't forget to serve with that pan sauce!

TIP

- If preparing a larger flank steak, adjust the cooking time. If your steak is between 1¾ and 2 pounds (795 and 900 g), I suggest a total broiling time of about 14 minutes.

almond-crusted chicken dinner

If you are new to breading chicken with almond flour, you are going to be so pleased with how these chicken cutlets turn out. Perfectly breaded and seasoned chicken with lemony asparagus deserves a place on your menu.

PREP TIME 10 minutes
TOTAL TIME 30 minutes
MAKES 4 servings

ALMOND-CRUSTED CHICKEN CUTLET

2 tablespoons (28 ml) extra-virgin olive oil

1¼ cups (140 g) finely ground almond flour

¾ teaspoon chili powder

¾ teaspoon garlic powder

¾ teaspoon dried parsley

¾ teaspoon dried basil

¾ teaspoon salt

2 large eggs

2 tablespoons (28 ml) coconut aminos

1 to 1½ pounds (455 to 680 g) chicken breast cutlets, thinly sliced

ASPARAGUS

1 bunch asparagus, trimmed (thick stalk works best)

1 tablespoon (15 ml) extra-virgin olive oil

Juice from ½ lemon

¼ teaspoon salt

1. Make the Almond-Crusted Chicken Cutlet: Preheat the oven to 450°F (230°C, or gas mark 8). Grease a 12 x 17-inch (30 x 43 cm) baking sheet with the oil.

2. In a shallow dish, combine the almond flour, chili powder, garlic powder, parsley, basil, and salt. Mix well.

3. In separate bowl, whisk together the eggs and coconut aminos.

4. Dredge each chicken cutlet in the egg mixture and let the excess drip off. Then, dredge each cutlet in the breading mixture.

5. Place each breaded cutlet on one side of the prepared baking sheet, leaving room for the asparagus later. Bake for 12 minutes.

6. Remove the pan from the oven. Carefully flip each cutlet. Be gentle so the breading doesn't stick to the pan.

7. Make the Asparagus: Add the asparagus beside the chicken. Drizzle with the oil and lemon juice. Sprinkle with the salt. Bake until the chicken is cooked through to a minimum internal temperature of 165°F (74°C), about 8 minutes more. (If using boneless pork chops, cook to a minimum internal temperature of 145°F [63°C].)

TIP

- To bread your chicken, lay a cutlet on top of the breading ingredients and use your fingers to cover the top of the cutlet with breading and press it into the chicken. Breading will stick to the bottom of your cutlet while you do this.
- Feel free to swap out the chicken for boneless pork chops.

turkey meatballs in marinara over butternut squash noodles

I'm a meatball junkie, which means I really think I could eat meatballs every day without growing bored. There are just so many ways to serve them up! This delightful meatball dinner is a bit different than your typical spaghetti and meatballs. It feels and tastes fresh because we are using minimal sauce and pairing the meatballs with thick butternut squash noodles—and it's all done on a sheet pan!

PREP TIME 15 minutes
TOTAL TIME 30 minutes
MAKES 4 servings

TURKEY MEATBALLS

1 pound (455 g) 93% lean ground turkey

¼ cup (28 g) almond flour

¼ cup (40 g) white or yellow onion, diced into ¼-inch (6 mm) pieces

¼ cup (16 g) finely chopped fresh parsley, plus more for garnish (optional)

1 large egg

1 tablespoon (10 g) minced garlic

1 teaspoon salt

½ teaspoon black pepper

½ teaspoon onion powder

EASY MARINARA SAUCE

16 ounces (455 g) canned tomato sauce

½ teaspoon salt

½ teaspoon dried basil

½ teaspoon dried oregano

BUTTERNUT SQUASH NOODLES

6 cups (about 22 ounces, or 625 g) butternut squash noodles

3 tablespoons (45 ml) extra-virgin olive oil

½ teaspoon salt

Chopped fresh basil, for garnish (optional)

1. Make the Turkey Meatballs: Preheat the oven to 450°F (230°C, or gas mark 8). Line a 12 x 17-inch (30 x 43 cm) baking sheet with parchment paper.

2. In a large bowl, combine the turkey, almond flour, onion, parsley, egg, garlic, salt, black pepper, and onion powder. Use a small cookie scoop or tablespoon to shape the meatballs. We want to keep them small (1 tablespoon [15 g] in size, or about 1 inch [2.5 cm]) so they'll cook quickly. You should have 20 to 22 meatballs. Lay them in a single layer on the prepared baking sheet, leaving a little space in between each.

3. Bake for 5 minutes.

4. Meanwhile, make the Easy Marinara Sauce: In a medium bowl, stir together the tomato sauce, salt, basil, and oregano.

5. Remove the baking sheet from the oven. Use a spatula or tongs to gently move the meatballs to one side of the pan. Pour the Easy Marinara Sauce over the meatballs.

6. Make the Butternut Squash Noodles: Spread the noodles on the open half of the baking sheet. Drizzle with the oil and sprinkle with the salt.

7. Bake until the meatballs are cooked through to a minimum internal temperature of 165°F (74°C) and the Butternut Squash Noodles are tender with a bit of crunch, 10 to 15 minutes.

8. Use tongs to add the Butternut Squash Noodles to each plate. Top with the meatballs and sauce. Garnish with additional fresh chopped parsley, or basil, if you like.

roasted cranberry chicken & brussels sprouts

Tart fresh cranberries burst as you roast them and add so much flavor to this chicken. I love it paired with crispy roasted Brussels sprouts! Cubed pork tenderloin would also be divine here, so feel free to swap out the chicken, if you want to change things up.

PREP TIME 10 minutes
TOTAL TIME 30 minutes
MAKES 6 to 8 servings

2 pounds (900 g) Brussels sprouts, trimmed and halved (if large)

12 ounces (340 g) fresh cranberries

4 tablespoons (60 ml) extra-virgin olive oil, divided

2 tablespoons (28 ml) pure maple syrup

2 tablespoons (28 ml) coconut aminos

2 pounds (900 g) boneless, skinless chicken breasts, cut into 1-inch (2.5 cm) pieces

1 tablespoon (2 g) finely chopped fresh rosemary

1½ teaspoons salt

1. Preheat the oven to 425°F (220°C, or gas mark 7). Line a 12 x 17-inch (30 x 43 cm) baking sheet with parchment paper.

2. Spread the Brussels sprouts and cranberries in an even layer on the prepared baking sheet. Drizzle 2 tablespoons (28 ml) of the oil over everything. Bake for 5 minutes.

3. Meanwhile, add the remaining 2 tablespoons (28 ml) oil, maple syrup, and coconut aminos to a small bowl. Stir until combined.

4. Remove the pan from the oven and add the chicken, mixing it in with the Brussels sprouts and cranberries. It's a tight fit, but it will fit. Pour the syrup mixture over everything and sprinkle with the rosemary and salt. Use a spatula to move the Brussels sprouts, cranberries, and chicken around so it's all well coated. Spread in an even layer.

5. Bake until the chicken is cooked through, completely opaque and juices run clear, about 15 minutes.

sheet-pan chicken cabbage stir-fry

A stir-fry prepared on a sheet pan? Yes, please! This stir-fry is fully loaded with cabbage, broccoli, Brussels sprouts, onion, and chicken. Roasting the veggies gives you all those crispy edges you love. Top with sriracha sauce for extra heat, and I swear you'll think it tastes like a classic pad Thai!

PREP TIME 10 minutes
TOTAL TIME 30 minutes
MAKES 4 servings

4 cups (280 g) shredded cabbage

2 cups (142 g) chopped broccoli

2 cups (176 g) Brussels sprouts, halved or quartered

½ white or yellow onion, thinly sliced

1 pound (455 g) chicken breasts, sliced into 1-inch (2.5 cm) pieces

2 tablespoons (28 ml) extra-virgin olive oil

1½ teaspoons minced garlic

½ teaspoon salt

½ teaspoon ground ginger

¼ cup (25 g) chopped scallions

3 tablespoons (45 ml) coconut aminos

Sriracha or hot sauce, for topping

1. Preheat the oven to 425°F (220°C, or gas mark 7).

2. Spread the cabbage, broccoli, Brussels sprouts, and onion on a 12 x 17-inch (30 x 43 cm) sheet pan. Add the chicken on top of the vegetables.

3. Drizzle the oil over everything. Add the garlic. Sprinkle with the salt and ginger.

4. Bake until the chicken is cooked through, completely opaque and juices run clear, and the veggies are tender with some crispiness, 20 to 25 minutes.

5. After roasting, add the scallions and coconut aminos. Stir to combine. Drizzle the sriracha or hot sauce over everything before serving.

TIP

- Sliced pork tenderloin would make an excellent substitution for the chicken, if that's what you have.

beef tips with veggies

Prepare yourself for one of my all-time favorites. This recipe was inspired by my mother-in-law, who always makes delicious beef tips. I've given it a Paleo spin and turned it into a one-pan meal by incorporating green beans. Make this recipe once, and you'll be making it a hundred times because it's just that good.

PREP TIME 10 minutes + marinating time
TOTAL TIME 25 minutes
MAKES 4 to 6 servings

MARINADE

¼ cup (60 ml) coconut aminos

¼ red (60 ml) wine vinegar

2 tablespoons (28 ml) extra-virgin olive oil

1 tablespoon (10 g) minced garlic

1 tablespoon (6 g) Italian seasoning

1 teaspoon salt

½ teaspoon black pepper

BEEF TIPS & VEGGIES

1½ pounds (680 g) top sirloin, sliced into strips ½ inch (1 cm) thick and 2 inches (5 cm) long

12 ounces (340 g) green beans, trimmed

1 white or yellow onion, cut into strips

1 green bell pepper, cut into strips

2½ tablespoons (40 ml) extra-virgin olive oil

½ teaspoon salt

1. Make the Marinade: In a resealable plastic bag or bowl, combine the marinade ingredients.

2. Make the Beef Tips & Veggies: Add the sirloin to the marinade, seal the bag, and toss to coat. Refrigerate for a minimum of 1 hour and up to 12 hours before cooking.

3. Set the oven rack to the middle position and turn the broiler on high.

4. Spread the green beans, onion, and bell pepper in a single layer on a 12 x 17-inch (30 x 43 cm) baking sheet. Drizzle with the oil and sprinkle with the salt. Broil for 10 minutes.

5. Add the marinated steak to the pan with your vegetables. Stir so that everything is in an even layer. If you have any marinade left, pour that in too. Broil until the steak is done to your liking, 4 to 5 minutes.

4

craveable skillet meals

It's hard to beat the easy cleanup and prep of skillet meals. They're perfect for busy weeknights because everything goes right in one pan—and you can even serve dinner from it!

20-minute skillet sausage & zucchini

Throw together this quick skillet dinner when you need a healthy and satisfying meal in a hurry! You'll love this perfectly seasoned mix of sausage, zucchini, peppers, and onions.

PREP TIME 10 minutes
TOTAL TIME 20 minutes
MAKES 4 servings

2½ tablespoons (40 ml) extra-virgin olive oil or avocado oil, divided

4 fully cooked sausages, sliced into circles ¼ inch (6 mm) thick

2 medium zucchini, diced into 1-inch (2 cm) pieces

1 white or yellow onion, diced into 1-inch (2 cm) pieces

1 bell pepper, any color, diced into 1-inch (2 cm) pieces

½ teaspoon salt

½ teaspoon dried oregano

½ teaspoon dried basil

¼ teaspoon garlic powder

¼ teaspoon onion powder

¼ teaspoon black pepper

1 teaspoon minced garlic

Fresh chopped basil, for garnish (optional)

1. Add 1 tablespoon (15 ml) of the oil to a skillet over medium-high heat. Once hot, add the sliced sausage. Sautè, flipping the sausage frequently, until the sausage has some browning, 2 to 3 minutes. Remove from the pan and set aside.

2. Reduce the heat to medium. Add the remaining 1½ tablespoons (25 ml) of oil to the skillet with the zucchini, onion, and bell pepper. Sprinkle with the salt, oregano, basil, garlic powder, onion powder, and black pepper. Stir. Sautè until the onion is translucent and the peppers and zucchini are close to tender, about 5 minutes.

3. Return the sausage to the skillet along with the minced garlic. Stir. Cover so everything heats through for 1 to 2 minutes. Taste and add more salt, if desired. Garnish with chopped fresh basil, if desired.

skillet chicken with summer vegetables

We always have way more squash and zucchini than I know what to do with by the end of summer. Our garden gives us an abundance, and it can get a bit out of hand! This skillet chicken is a delicious way to enjoy our favorite summer veggies. It's an easy dish made of fresh ingredients.

PREP TIME 10 minutes
TOTAL TIME 25 minutes
MAKES 2 to 4 servings

2 boneless, skinless chicken breasts (½ pound, or 225 g each)

2 teaspoons dried basil

1 teaspoon garlic powder, divided

1 teaspoon salt, divided

½ teaspoon onion powder

3 tablespoons (45 ml) extra-virgin olive oil or avocado oil, divided

2 yellow squash, halved and sliced into half-moons

2 medium zucchini, halved and sliced into half-moons

½ white or yellow onion, diced into ½-inch (1 cm) pieces

1 tablespoon (4 g) chopped fresh parsley

1. Slice the chicken horizontally to create four thin cutlets. Season all sides with the basil, ½ teaspoon of the garlic powder, ½ teaspoon of the salt, and onion powder.

2. Add 1 tablespoon (15 ml) of the oil to a skillet over medium-high heat. Place the cutlets in the hot pan. (You should hear a little sizzle.) Cook until browned, 3 to 4 minutes. Flip and brown the other side, another 3 to 4 minutes.

3. Carefully move the chicken to one side of the skillet and reduce the heat to medium. Add the remaining 2 tablespoons (28 ml) oil, squash, zucchini, and onion. Sprinkle with the remaining ½ teaspoon salt and remaining ½ teaspoon garlic powder. Cover and simmer, stirring the veggies occasionally, until the vegetables are tender and the chicken is cooked through to a minimum internal temperature of 165°F (74°C), 5 to 7 minutes. (If using pork cutlets, cook to a minimum internal temperature of 145°F [63°C].)

4. Garnish with the parsley before serving. Taste and add salt, if desired.

TIP

- Swap out the chicken for thin-sliced pork cutlets, if you like.

fiesta pineapple chicken

This easy stir-fry of chicken, pineapple, and vegetables is the perfect combination of sweet and savory. It's also so pretty, if I do say so myself!

PREP TIME 10 minutes
TOTAL TIME 25 minutes
MAKES 4 servings

2 tablespoons (28 ml) extra-virgin olive oil or avocado oil

1 pound (455 g) boneless, skinless chicken breasts, cut into 1-inch (2.5 cm) pieces

1 red bell pepper, cut into 1-inch (2.5 cm) pieces

½ white or yellow onion, cut into 1-inch (2.5 cm) pieces

12 ounces (340 g) green beans, trimmed and halved

¾ teaspoon salt

½ teaspoon black pepper

½ teaspoon ground ginger

1 can (14 ounces, or 390 g) pineapple chunks, drained, or 1½ cups (250 g) fresh

½ cup (120 ml) chicken stock

¼ cup (60 ml) coconut aminos

1½ teaspoons minced garlic

¼ teaspoon crushed red pepper flakes

1 tablespoon (9 g) arrowroot flour

1 tablespoon (15 ml) cold water

1. Add the oil to the skillet over medium-high heat. Once hot, add the chicken. Sauté, flipping occasionally to brown all sides of the chicken, about 3 to 5 minutes, using a spatula to separate the pieces when they get stuck together. Remove the chicken from the skillet and set aside.

2. Add the bell pepper, onion, and green beans to the skillet. Sauté, stirring occasionally, until the onion is tender and the bell pepper and green beans have some browning, about 5 minutes.

3. Add the chicken back to your skillet along with the salt, black pepper, and ginger. Stir in the pineapple chunks.

4. Stir in the stock, coconut aminos, garlic, and red pepper flakes. Simmer for 2 to 3 minutes until the chicken is cooked through, completely opaque and juices run clear, and everything is warmed through.

5. Turn off the stove. To thicken the sauce, combine the arrowroot flour and water in a small jar. Shake vigorously and pour the slurry into the skillet and stir. The sauce will begin to thicken immediately.

6. Taste and add more salt and black pepper, if desired.

paleo tuna poke

This is likely my husband's favorite recipe. It is super simple to throw together and so ridiculously flavorful! The only cooking this dish requires is in preparing the cauliflower rice. Here, I'm showing you how to steam it in a skillet, but you are welcome to buy the cauliflower rice that steams in a bag and use that to further simplify things. This recipe is made to feed one person (it's a generous serving), so double it or triple it depending on how many you are serving.

PREP TIME 15 minutes
TOTAL TIME 20 minutes
MAKES 1 serving

CAULIFLOWER RICE

2 cups (8 ounces, or 225 g) cauliflower rice

1 tablespoon (15 ml) extra-virgin olive oil

Salt and black pepper, to taste

SPICY MAYO

2 tablespoons (28 g) mayo

1 teaspoon sriracha or hot sauce

TUNA & VEGGIES & SESAME-SOY SAUCE

3 ounces (85 g) sushi-grade tuna, cut into ½-inch (1 cm) cubes

½ cup (70 g) diced cucumber, ½-inch (1 cm) cubes

¼ cup (35 g) shredded purple cabbage

¼ cup (28 g) grated carrot

¼ cup (21 g) microgreens

3 tablespoons (45 ml) coconut aminos

1½ teaspoons extra-virgin olive oil

1 teaspoon rice vinegar

½ avocado, sliced

Sesame seeds, for garnish

1. Make the Cauliflower Rice: Add the cauliflower to a skillet over medium heat with the oil. Cover with a lid so the cauliflower steams until tender, 4 to 5 minutes. (If you're doubling or tripling this recipe, your cauliflower will take a few more minutes to cook.) Add salt and black pepper, to taste.

2. Meanwhile, prepare the Spicy Mayo: In a small bowl, stir together the mayo and sriracha or hot sauce.

3. Make the Tuna & Veggies & Sesame-Soy Sauce: In a medium bowl, gently toss together the tuna, cucumber, cabbage, carrots, and microgreens. Drizzle the coconut aminos, oil, and vinegar over the top. Stir so everything is coated.

4. To serve, layer the cauliflower rice in the bottom of a bowl. Top with your tuna and veggie mixture. Add your Spicy Mayo and sliced avocado on top. Now, garnish with sesame seeds.

chicken squash skillet

Fresh zucchini and butternut squash make this skillet meal a celebration of fall veggies. Swap out the chicken for pork tenderloin, if you like, and serve it all over cauliflower rice to take full advantage of the sauce.

PREP TIME 10 minutes
TOTAL TIME 25 minutes
MAKES 4 servings

1½ tablespoons (25 ml) extra-virgin olive oil or avocado oil

1 yellow or orange bell pepper, cut into strips

½ white or yellow onion, cut into strips

1 teaspoon minced garlic

1 pound (455 g) boneless, skinless chicken breasts, cut into thin pieces

2 medium zucchini, halved and sliced into half-moons (about 3 cups, or 360 g)

2 cups (280 g) diced butternut squash, 1-inch (2.5 cm) cubes (see Tip)

¾ cup (175 ml) chicken stock

¼ cup (60 ml) coconut aminos

1 tablespoon (15 ml) rice vinegar

¾ teaspoon salt

½ teaspoon black pepper

¼ teaspoon ground ginger

¼ teaspoon crushed red pepper flakes

1. Add the oil to a large skillet over medium-high heat. Once hot, add the bell pepper and onion. Sauté until the pepper has a bit of browning and the onion is tender, 3 to 4 minutes. Add the garlic and sauté for another minute so the garlic is golden in color. Remove from the pan and set aside.

2. Add the chicken to the skillet. (If needed, drizzle in another tablespoon [15 ml] oil.) Sauté, stirring frequently, until the chicken is nicely browned, about 3 minutes. It doesn't need to be fully cooked through at this point; we're just adding a bit of color to our chicken.

3. Add the zucchini, butternut squash, stock, coconut aminos, vinegar, salt, black pepper, ginger, red pepper flakes, and the cooked bell pepper and onion to the skillet. Stir. Reduce the heat to medium, cover, and simmer until the zucchini and squash are tender and the chicken is cooked through, completely opaque and juices run clear, 5 to 10 minutes. Taste and add more salt and black pepper, if desired.

TIP

- While I always slice up my own zucchini and yellow squash, I'm a big fan of purchasing the cubed butternut squash from the grocery store. It saves some trouble and time. Plus, butternut squash can be fairly large, and I rarely want to use an entire squash of that size. Whether to chop or not is totally your call!

stuffed pizza chicken with veggies

Stuff your chicken breasts with a mix of mushrooms, bell pepper, and diced pepperoni to emulate a supreme pizza. It looks impressive, especially when paired with sautéed green beans!

PREP TIME 10 minutes
TOTAL TIME 30 minutes
MAKES 4 servings

CHICKEN

4 boneless, skinless chicken breasts (½ pound, or 225 g, each)

2 tablespoons (28 ml) extra-virgin olive oil or avocado oil, plus more for drizzling

1½ tablespoons (9 g) Italian seasoning

¾ teaspoon salt

PIZZA FILLING

1 tablespoon (15 ml) extra-virgin olive oil or avocado oil

½ cup (35 g) chopped fresh mushrooms

½ cup (75 g) diced bell pepper of any color, ½-inch (1 cm) pieces

30 pieces pepperoni (about 2 ounces, or 55 g), diced

GREEN BEANS

2 tablespoons (28 ml) extra-virgin olive oil or avocado oil

12 ounces (340 g) green beans, trimmed

¼ teaspoon salt

1. Make the Chicken: Slice each chicken breast on the side, about halfway through, to create a pocket for the stuffing. Drizzle a little oil all over the chicken breasts and sprinkle with the Italian seasoning and salt.

2. Make the Pizza Filling: Add the oil to a large skillet over medium-high heat. Once hot, add the mushrooms and bell pepper. Sauté, stirring occasionally, until the peppers soften and have some browning, 3 to 5 minutes.

3. Transfer the mushrooms and bell peppers to a small bowl and stir in the pepperoni. Set aside.

4. Add 2 tablespoons (28 ml) oil to the skillet and return to medium-high heat. Carefully stuff the filling inside the chicken pockets. Place in the skillet, top-side down. Let the chicken cook undisturbed until golden brown, 2 to 3 minutes. Flip and cook until the other side is browned, another 2 to 3 minutes. The chicken will not be cooked through at this point. Remove the chicken from the skillet and set aside.

5. Make the Green Beans: Add the oil to your skillet along with the green beans. Reduce the heat to medium. Cook, stirring occasionally, until they start to soften and you see some browning, 5 to 7 minutes. Sprinkle with the salt.

6. Use a spatula or tongs to gently move the green beans to one side of the skillet. Add the chicken back to the skillet beside the green beans. Cover and cook for 5 to 10 minutes, or until the chicken is cooked through.

7. Check to make sure the chicken is cooked through to a minimum internal temperature of 165°F (74°C). Taste and add more salt or black pepper, if desired.

orange-balsamic chicken with broccoli

Orange and balsamic are a fun and surprising flavor combination that I can't get enough of. It all started with a recipe I made a few years ago for orange-balsamic chicken wings, and my immensely popular orange-balsamic meatballs came next. Now, I'm letting that duo shine in this quick chicken and broccoli stir-fry. If you prefer pork tenderloin or boneless pork chops, they'd make a fine substitute for the chicken.

PREP TIME 10 minutes
TOTAL TIME 20 minutes
MAKES 2 servings

2 tablespoons (28 ml) extra-virgin olive oil or avocado oil

1½ pounds (680 g) boneless, skinless chicken breasts, cut into 1-inch (2.5 cm) pieces

Zest from 1 orange

½ cup (120 ml) fresh orange juice

2 tablespoons (28 ml) pure maple syrup

2 tablespoons (28 ml) balsamic vinegar

1 teaspoon tomato paste

1 teaspoon salt

½ teaspoon ground ginger

½ teaspoon garlic powder

½ teaspoon black pepper

12 ounces (340 g) broccoli florets

1. Add the oil to a skillet over medium-high heat. Once hot, add the chicken. Sauté, stirring frequently, until the chicken is nicely browned and cooked through, completely opaque and juices run clear, 3 to 5 minutes. It cooks quickly because it's been cut into small pieces.

2. Add the zest, orange juice, maple syrup, vinegar, tomato paste, salt, ginger, garlic powder, and black pepper to the skillet. Stir to combine. Now, add the broccoli. Cover and let your broccoli steam until it's how you like it, usually 2 to 3 minutes to keep it bright with a little crispiness.

3. Once done simmering, turn off the heat and uncover. Let sit for 2 minutes to cook off a bit of the sauce. Taste and add more salt and black pepper, if desired.

garlic-lemon halibut with sautéed asparagus

Halibut has a mild flavor that pleases pretty much everybody. (Even those who protest that they don't really enjoy seafood.) My favorite way to dress it up is with a lovely sauce of ghee, lemon juice, garlic, and thyme. It's just perfect with asparagus!

PREP TIME 5 minutes
TOTAL TIME 10 minutes
MAKES 4 servings

HALIBUT & ASPARAGUS

4 halibut fillets (6 ounces, or 170 g, each)

Salt and black pepper

2 tablespoons (28 ml) extra-virgin olive oil

1 bunch asparagus, trimmed

GARLIC-LEMON SAUCE

¼ cup (56 g) ghee, melted

2 tablespoons (28 ml) fresh lemon juice

1 tablespoon (2 g) chopped fresh thyme

1 teaspoon minced garlic

1. Make the Halibut & Asparagus: Generously sprinkle the top and bottom of the halibut with salt and black pepper.

2. Add the oil to a large skillet over medium-high heat. Once hot, carefully add each fillet with the presentation-side down. Place the asparagus beside the fish and sprinkle with salt. We want a beautiful golden color on the side of the halibut that's touching the bottom of the pan, so don't flip it until you've achieved that color, 4 to 5 minutes.

3. Meanwhile, make the Garlic-Lemon Sauce: Stir together the ghee, lemon juice, thyme, and garlic in a small bowl.

4. Carefully flip your halibut and use your spatula or tongs to move the asparagus around so all the stalks get a turn at the bottom of the pan.

5. Reduce the heat to medium-low or low. Pour your ghee mixture over the halibut and asparagus. Cover and let the halibut cook through until it is opaque and flakes easily with a fork, 3 to 4 minutes.

6. To serve, divide the asparagus among plates and top with the halibut. Drizzle a bit of the sauce from the pan over the fish.

spanish chicken

My obsession with ghee is real and has been going for 5+ years! It is my go-to cooking fat for chicken because it adds a hint of sweetness and helps everything brown beautifully. It's the ghee, along with the bold flavors in the dry rub, that make this chicken extra delicious.

PREP TIME 10 minutes
TOTAL TIME 25 minutes
MAKES 2 to 4 servings

DRY RUB

1 teaspoon paprika

¾ teaspoon salt

½ teaspoon garlic powder

½ teaspoon onion powder

½ teaspoon ground cumin

½ teaspoon chili powder

CHICKEN & VEGGIES

2 boneless, skinless chicken breasts (½ pound, or 225 g, each)

2½ tablespoons (35 g) ghee, divided

8 ounces (225 g) green beans, trimmed

Handful of cherry tomatoes

½ teaspoon salt

1. Make the Dry Rub: Combine the paprika, salt, garlic powder, onion powder, cumin, and chili powder in a small bowl.

2. Make the Chicken & Veggies: Slice the chicken horizontally to create four thin cutlets. Press the Dry Rub into the top of the cutlets.

3. Add 1½ tablespoons (21 g) of the ghee to a skillet over medium-high heat. Once hot, add the chicken, seasoned-side down. (You should hear a little sizzle.) Cook until browned, 3 to 4 minutes. Flip and brown the other side, another 3 to 4 minutes. Your seasoned side will have significantly more browning thanks to that incredible dry rub.

4. Carefully move the chicken to one side of the skillet and reduce the heat to medium. Add the remaining 1 tablespoon (14 g) ghee, green beans, and tomatoes to the other side of the skillet. Add the salt to the veggies. Cover and simmer until the chicken is cooked through, completely opaque and juices run clear, and the green beans are tender with some crunch, 5 to 10 minutes.

skillet chicken & brussels sprouts

Whip up this simple stir-fry of chicken and Brussels sprouts any night of the week in only 25 minutes! It sautés in an easy sauce of coconut aminos, rice vinegar, garlic, and crushed red pepper flakes to infuse every bite with big flavor. Feel free to swap the chicken with pork tenderloin.

PREP TIME 10 minutes
TOTAL TIME 25 minutes
MAKES 2 to 4 servings

1½ tablespoons (25 ml) extra-virgin olive oil or avocado oil

1½ pounds (680 g) boneless, skinless chicken breasts, cut into 1-inch (2.5 cm) pieces

1 pound (455 g) Brussels sprouts, trimmed and halved

Salt and black pepper

½ cup (120 ml) coconut aminos

1 tablespoon (15 ml) rice vinegar or apple cider vinegar

1 tablespoon (10 g) minced garlic

¼ to ½ teaspoon crushed red pepper flakes

1. Add the oil to a large skillet over medium-high heat. Once hot, add the chicken and Brussels sprouts. Sprinkle with salt and black pepper. Sauté for 3 to 4 minutes, stirring occasionally. The chicken should be close to done with some color, and the Brussels sprouts will have a bit of brown. Use a spatula to gently separate the chicken that gets stuck together.

2. Stir in the coconut aminos, vinegar, garlic, and red pepper flakes. Reduce the heat to medium and cover. Simmer until the Brussels sprouts are softened and the chicken is cooked all the way through, completely opaque and juices run clear, 5 to 6 minutes.

3. Turn off the heat and uncover. Let sit for 2 minutes to cook off a bit of the sauce. Taste and add extra salt or black pepper, if desired.

TIP

- This is a delicious meal on its own, but if you'd like to make it even heartier, simply serve it over steamed cauliflower rice or roasted veggies and potatoes.

crispy chicken thighs with greens

Get your greens in this simple dish of lightly spiced chicken thighs and garlicky spinach. You can swap out the spinach for any other fast-cooking green veggie and make this seem like a new dish every time you make it!

PREP TIME 5 minutes
TOTAL TIME 20 minutes
MAKES 4 servings

CHICKEN THIGHS

½ teaspoon salt

½ teaspoon chili powder

½ teaspoon garlic powder

½ teaspoon black pepper

¼ teaspoon curry powder

¼ teaspoon paprika

1½ pounds (680 g) boneless, skinless chicken thighs

1½ tablespoons (21 g) ghee (see Tip)

SPINACH

½ to 1½ teaspoons extra-virgin olive oil

15 ounces (425 g) fresh baby spinach (see Tip)

1½ teaspoons minced garlic

½ teaspoon salt

1. Make the Chicken Thighs: In a small bowl, stir together the salt, chili powder, garlic powder, black pepper, curry powder, and paprika.

2. Pat the chicken thighs dry. Rub the spice mixture into the top of the chicken.

3. Place the ghee in a skillet over medium-high heat. Once hot, add the chicken, seasoned-side down. (You should hear a sizzle.) Flip once you see a beautiful brown on the side of the chicken in the pan, 5 minutes. Brown the other side, another 6 to 7 minutes. Remove the chicken from the pan and set aside.

4. Make the Spinach: Reduce the heat to medium. Assess how much fat remains in the skillet. You may find that you don't need to add any oil, or you may only need a little. Add the oil (if needed), spinach, garlic, and salt. Stir until all the spinach fits. Place the chicken thighs on top of the spinach. Cover and simmer until the chicken is cooked through to a minimum internal temperature of 165°F (74°C) and the spinach is wilted, 2 to 4 minutes.

TIP

- Use another cooking fat in place of ghee if you like. I personally really enjoy the rich flavor of ghee for sautéing chicken.

- Interested in using something other than spinach? Mustard greens cook quickly, so they're a great swap; tear or chop the greens into large pieces before sautéing. If you'd like to use kale, remove the thickest part of the stems first and then give the leaves a rough chop; cook kale for 6 to 8 minutes. Broccoli cooks fast, too; just move those thighs to the side of your skillet, add the broccoli, and cover and cook until it's how you like it!

alfredo chicken & zoodles

A creamy yet dairy-free alfredo sauce makes this dish really shine. The nutritional yeast gives it that cheesy flavor, while the cashews make it silky and lush. With chicken, asparagus, and zoodles, this is one comfort food that's actually light!

PREP TIME 15 minutes + cashew soak time
TOTAL TIME 30 minutes
MAKES 4 servings

ALFREDO SAUCE

1 cup (140 g) raw cashews (see Tip)

1½ tablespoons (25 ml) extra-virgin olive oil

½ white onion, diced into ½-inch (1 cm) pieces

1 tablespoon (10 g) minced garlic

1½ tablespoons (25 ml) fresh lemon juice

1 tablespoon (4 g) nutritional yeast

1 teaspoon salt

½ teaspoon black pepper

CHICKEN & ASPARAGUS

2 tablespoons (28 ml) extra-virgin olive oil or avocado oil

1 pound (455 g) boneless, skinless chicken breasts, cut into 1-inch (2.5 cm) pieces

½ bunch asparagus, trimmed and cut into thirds

½ teaspoon salt

ZOODLES

4 medium zucchini, or 20 ounces (560 g) store-bought zoodles

1. Make the Alfredo Sauce: Soak the cashews in water to cover for at least 1 hour. Drain the water when you're ready to cook.

2. Add the oil to a skillet over medium-high heat. Once hot, add the onion. Sauté until tender, 3 to 4 minutes. Add the garlic and sauté until golden, another minute.

3. Transfer the mixture to a high-powered blender or food processor, along with the soaked cashews, ¾ cup (175 ml) water, the lemon juice, nutritional yeast, salt, and black pepper. Blend until smooth. Taste and add more salt or black pepper, if desired.

4. Make the Chicken & Asparagus: Add the oil to the skillet over medium-high heat. Sauté the chicken to brown all sides, about 3 minutes, using a spatula to separate the pieces when they get stuck together. Add the asparagus and sauté until the asparagus is crisp tender and the chicken is cooked through, about 3 minutes. Add the salt to the chicken and asparagus.

5. Meanwhile, prepare your Zoodles: Make zucchini noodles from the zucchini using a spiralizer according to the manufacturer's directions.

6. Reduce the heat to medium-low. Pour your Alfredo Sauce into the skillet. Use tongs to stir in the zoodles, cover, and simmer until the zoodles are how you like them. This can take as little as 2 minutes, if you're using the thin store-bought zoodles, or as long as 5 minutes, if you make your own thick zoodles (my preference).

TIP

- To soften cashews quickly, add the cashews to a bowl, add water to cover, and microwave for about 1 minute.

5

stovetop soups

There is nothing like a bowl of soup to warm you from the inside out. Unfortunately, so many soups call for you to slowly simmer until the end of time. I am of the opinion that it is possible to bring out tons of flavor without that eternal simmering, so the soups you'll find in this chapter are fast, my friend.

chicken curry soup

Craving all the flavor of curry but want it fast? This soup features a creamy curry broth, chicken, bell peppers, and sweet potato. It's a simple dish that packs tons of flavor.

PREP TIME 10 minutes
TOTAL TIME 30 minutes
MAKES 6 to 8 servings

2 tablespoons (28 ml) extra-virgin olive oil or avocado oil

2 red bell peppers, diced into ½-inch (1 cm) pieces

1 white or yellow onion, diced into ½-inch (1 cm) pieces

1 teaspoon minced garlic

1½ pounds (680 g) boneless, skinless chicken breasts, cut into 1-inch (2.5 cm) pieces

2 cups (266 g) diced sweet potatoes, 1-inch (2.5 cm) cubes

32 ounces (946 ml) chicken stock

1 can (14.5 ounces, or 410 g) diced tomatoes

¼ cup (64 g) tomato paste

1 tablespoon (6 g) curry powder

1 teaspoon ground ginger

1 teaspoon salt

½ teaspoon cayenne pepper

¼ teaspoon ground cumin

¼ teaspoon coriander

1 can (13.5 ounces, or 380 g) unsweetened full-fat coconut milk

Fresh cilantro, chopped

1. Add the oil to your soup pot over medium-high heat. Once hot, add the bell peppers and onion. Sauté until the onion is tender, 3 to 5 minutes. Add the garlic and sauté for another minute so the garlic is golden in color.

2. Add the chicken, sweet potatoes, stock, tomatoes, tomato paste, curry powder, ginger, salt, cayenne pepper, cumin, and coriander. Bring to a boil over high heat. Cover and reduce the heat to medium. Simmer until the chicken is cooked through and the sweet potato is tender, 15 to 20 minutes.

3. Remove from the heat and stir in the coconut milk. Top with fresh chopped cilantro when you're ready to serve!

no-bean 30-minute chili

This yummy chili is thick. It's hearty. It's dark. It doesn't have beans, but you're not going to notice. It's a chili you are going to want to make on a regular basis.

PREP TIME 5 minutes
TOTAL TIME 30 minutes
MAKES 6 to 8 servings

- 2 pounds (900 g) lean ground beef or turkey
- 1 green bell pepper, finely chopped
- 1 large yellow onion, finely chopped
- 2 cans (14.5 ounces, or 410 g, each) diced tomatoes
- 2 cups (475 ml) beef stock
- 1 can (6 ounces, or 170 g) tomato paste
- ¼ cup (40 g) minced garlic
- 1½ tablespoons (12 g) chili powder
- 1½ teaspoons paprika
- 1½ teaspoons onion powder
- 1½ teaspoons salt
- 1 teaspoon garlic powder
- 1 teaspoon ground cumin
- 1 teaspoon black pepper
- Sliced scallions, diced onion, chopped avocado, or chopped cilantro, for garnish

1. Add the ground beef or turkey to a soup pot over medium-high heat. Use a spatula to crumble.

2. Add the bell pepper and onion. Cook, stirring occasionally, until the beef is browned and the veggies are softened, about 5 minutes.

3. Add the tomatoes, stock, tomato paste, garlic, chili powder, paprika, onion powder, salt, garlic powder, cumin, and black pepper. Stir. Reduce the heat to medium, cover, and simmer until the flavors marry, about 20 minutes.

4. Taste and add extra salt or black pepper, if you like. Serve with desired toppings.

TIP

- If your meat isn't very lean, you'll want to drain the grease after browning it. I use a 93% lean beef, so I don't drain mine.

beef stroganoff soup

This soup has all the flavor of a classic beef stroganoff, but it's oh so much lighter! It's rich, creamy, and tastes like it has been simmering for ages. I can't wait for you to try it!

PREP TIME 5 minutes
TOTAL TIME 30 minutes
MAKES 6 to 8 servings

1 tablespoon (15 ml) extra-virgin olive oil or ghee (For dairy-free dishes, use extra-virgin olive oil.)

1 pound (455 g) sirloin steak, sliced into small pieces

8 ounces (225 g) sliced mushrooms

½ white or yellow onion, diced into ½-inch (1 cm) pieces

2 teaspoons minced garlic

32 ounces (946 ml) beef stock

⅔ cup (160 ml) unsweetened, full-fat coconut milk, stirred

1 teaspoon balsamic vinegar

¾ teaspoon salt

½ teaspoon black pepper

½ teaspoon dried thyme

2 cups (8 ounces, or 225 g) cauliflower rice

1. Add the oil or ghee to your soup pot over medium-high heat. Once hot, add the steak, mushrooms, onion, and garlic. Sauté until the onion becomes tender and the steak is beautifully browned, about 5 minutes.

2. Add the stock, coconut milk, vinegar, salt, black pepper, and thyme. Cover, reduce the heat to medium, and simmer for 10 minutes.

3. Stir in the cauliflower rice. Cover and continue to simmer until the cauliflower is tender, another 10 minutes.

TIP

- The coconut milk helps create a creaminess in this soup that's reminiscent of traditional beef stroganoff. You will not taste any coconut in this dish since we're not using much, and I've paired it with plenty of other bold flavors that overpower it.

chicken sausage gumbo soup

I grew up in Mississippi, and our proximity to Louisiana meant gumbo was always available. My version of the New Orleans classic is a soup that's packed with chicken, okra, onion, bell pepper, celery, and lots of seasonings. It's a dish that's big on taste but ready in no time at all! I guarantee nobody will realize this is a healthy version!

PREP TIME 10 minutes
TOTAL TIME 30 minutes
MAKES 6 to 8 servings

2 tablespoons (28 ml) extra-virgin olive oil or ghee (For dairy-free dishes, use extra-virgin olive oil.)

1 white or yellow onion, diced into ½-inch (1 cm) pieces

1 cup (120 g) diced celery, ½-inch (1 cm) dice

1 green bell pepper, diced into ½-inch (1 cm) pieces

1 tablespoon (10 g) minced garlic

32 ounces (946 ml) chicken stock

1 pound (455 g) boneless, skinless chicken breasts, cut into 1-inch (2.5 cm) pieces

1 can (14.5 ounces, or 410 g) diced tomatoes

½ pound (225 g) okra, sliced into 1-inch (2.5 cm) pieces

2 precooked chicken sausages, sliced

1 bay leaf

½ teaspoon dried thyme

½ teaspoon dried basil

½ teaspoon salt

½ teaspoon black pepper

¼ teaspoon cayenne pepper

3 cups (12 ounces, or 340 g) fresh or frozen cauliflower rice

1. Add the oil or ghee to your soup pot over medium-high heat. Once hot, add the onion, celery, bell pepper, and garlic. Sauté until the onion becomes tender and fragrant, 3 to 4 minutes.

2. Add the stock, chicken, tomatoes, okra, sausages, bay leaf, thyme, basil, salt, black pepper, and cayenne pepper. Bring to a boil over high heat. Cover, reduce the heat to medium, and simmer for 10 minutes.

3. Stir in the cauliflower rice. Cover and continue to simmer until the cauliflower is tender and the chicken cooked through, another 8 to 10 minutes. Remove the bay leaf before serving.

beef "barley" soup

Is there barley in here? No, it's cauliflower rice! It's a perfect swap because it really looks so much like barley and absorbs whatever flavors you cook it with. Steak, veggies, and a tasty broth make this soup a complete meal.

PREP TIME 5 minutes
TOTAL TIME 30 minutes
MAKES 6 to 8 servings

1½ tablespoons (25 ml) extra-virgin olive oil or ghee (For dairy-free dishes, use extra-virgin olive oil.)

1 to 1½ pounds (455 to 680 g) sirloin steak, sliced into small pieces

½ white or yellow onion, diced into ½-inch (1 cm) pieces

1 cup (120 g) diced celery, ½-inch (1 cm) dice

1 cup (70 g) sliced mushrooms

1 cup (122 g) peeled, sliced carrots, ¼-inch (6 mm)-thick slices

1 tablespoon (10 g) minced garlic

32 ounces (946 ml) beef stock

2 tablespoons (32 g) tomato paste

2 tablespoons (28 ml) balsamic vinegar

2 teaspoons salt

1½ teaspoons black pepper

1 teaspoon dried thyme

1 teaspoon dried rosemary

1 teaspoon dried oregano

3 cups (12 ounces, or 340 g) fresh or frozen cauliflower rice

1. Add the oil or ghee and steak to your soup pot over medium-high heat. Brown all sides of the steak pieces, 3 to 4 minutes. Remove from the pot and set aside.

2. Add the onion, celery, mushrooms, carrots, and garlic to the pot. You should have enough fat from the beef already remaining, but add another 1½ teaspoons oil if not. Sauté until the onion becomes tender and fragrant, about 4 minutes.

3. Add the steak back to the pot along with the stock, tomato paste, vinegar, salt, black pepper, thyme, rosemary, and oregano. Reduce the heat to medium, cover, and simmer for 10 minutes.

4. Stir in the cauliflower rice. Cover and simmer until the cauliflower is soft, 8 to 10 minutes.

easiest vegetable soup

A truly delicious homemade vegetable soup doesn't need any meat at all. Mine is full of fresh veggies, including green beans, carrots, and sweet potatoes. They're swimming in a rich broth that will keep you coming back for more.

PREP TIME 10 minutes
TOTAL TIME 30 minutes
MAKES 6 to 8 servings

1 tablespoon (15 ml) extra-virgin olive oil or avocado oil

½ large white or yellow onion, diced into ½-inch (1 cm) pieces

1 teaspoon minced garlic

32 ounces (946 ml) chicken or vegetable stock (For vegan and vegetarian dishes, use vegetable stock.)

1 can (14.5 ounces, or 410 g) diced tomatoes

1 cup (100 g) chopped green beans

1 cup (122 g) peeled, sliced carrots, ¼-inch (6 mm)-thick slices

1 cup (133 g) diced sweet potatoes, ½-inch (1 cm) cubes

½ teaspoon salt

½ teaspoon black pepper

1 packed cup (about half a 5-ounce, or 140 g, package) baby spinach

¼ cup (15 g) chopped fresh parsley

1. Add the oil to your soup pot over medium to medium-high heat. Once the oil is hot, add the onion and sauté until softened, 3 to 4 minutes. Add the garlic and sauté for another minute so the garlic is golden in color.

2. Add the stock, tomatoes, green beans, carrots, sweet potatoes, salt, and black pepper. Bring to a boil over high heat. Cover, reduce the heat to medium, and simmer until the veggies are tender, 15 to 20 minutes.

3. Stir in the spinach and parsley. They will wilt right away. Taste and add extra salt or black pepper, if desired.

creamy seafood bisque

This creamy seafood bisque is one of my husband's favorites, and if you're a seafood lover, it's sure to be high on your list too! It looks and tastes like it's full of cream, but it's not. Instead, we use blended cauliflower and coconut milk to re-create that creaminess we associate with an amazing bisque. Use whatever seafood you like (I use a mixture of cod and shrimp) and adjust the hot sauce to your liking.

PREP TIME 10 minutes
TOTAL TIME 25 minutes
MAKES 6 servings

2 tablespoons (28 g) ghee or (28 ml) extra-virgin olive oil (For dairy-free dishes, use extra-virgin olive oil.)

3 cups (12 ounces, or 340 g) fresh or frozen cauliflower rice

½ white or yellow onion, coarsely chopped

2 ribs celery, chopped (about ¾ cup, or 75 g)

1 tablespoon (10 g) minced garlic

3 cups (700 ml) chicken or vegetable stock

1 cup (235 ml) canned unsweetened full-fat coconut milk, stirred

1½ teaspoons hot sauce (see Tip)

1½ teaspoons salt

1 teaspoon Old Bay seasoning

1 teaspoon dried thyme

1 to 1½ pounds (455 to 680 g) seafood

1. Add the ghee or oil to a soup pot over medium-high heat. Once hot, add the cauliflower rice, onion, celery, and garlic. Cover and cook, stirring occasionally, until the cauliflower and onion are tender, 6 to 8 minutes.

2. Transfer the mixture to a high-powered blender along with the stock and coconut milk. Blend until smooth. Alternatively, you can use an immersion blender to purée the mixture right in the soup pot.

3. If using a high-powered blender, pour the blended soup back into your pot. Add the hot sauce, salt, Old Bay, and thyme. Bring to a simmer over medium heat. Stir in your seafood and simmer until cooked through, 3 to 4 minutes.

TIP

- This soup has a little heat, so reduce the amount of hot sauce you use if that's your preference.

chicken zoodle soup

This chicken zoodle soup feels exactly like a traditional chicken noodle soup, even though there's nary a noodle in there. Think about it. When you're eating chicken noodle soup, you're not tasting the noodles, are you? Nope! It's all about that broth, tender vegetables, and chunks of chicken. This soup gives you all of that and still remains very light! It's perfect for a chilly evening at home.

PREP TIME 10 minutes
TOTAL TIME 30 minutes
MAKES 8 to 10 servings

1½ tablespoons (25 ml) extra-virgin olive oil or avocado oil

5 large carrots, peeled and chopped into ½-inch (1 cm) pieces

3 ribs celery, diced into ½-inch (1 cm) pieces

1 medium white or yellow onion, diced into ½-inch (1 cm) pieces

1 tablespoon (10 g) minced garlic

64 ounces (1.9 L) chicken stock

3 pounds (1.4 kg) boneless, skinless chicken breasts, cut into 1-inch (2.5 cm) pieces

¾ teaspoon salt

½ teaspoon black pepper

½ teaspoon garlic powder

4 to 6 medium zucchini, or 20 ounces (560 g) store-bought zoodles (see Tip)

½ cup (8 g) chopped fresh cilantro or (30 g) parsley

1. Add the oil to a soup pot over medium-high heat. Once hot, add the carrots, celery, onion, and garlic. Sauté until the onion is tender, stirring occasionally, about 5 minutes. (The carrots do not need to be completely cooked through at this point.)

2. Add the stock, chicken, salt, black pepper, and garlic powder. Bring to a simmer. Reduce the heat to medium, cover, and cook until the chicken is cooked through, completely opaque and juices run clear, 15 to 20 minutes.

3. While the soup is simmering, prepare the zoodles. Make zucchini noodles from the zucchini using a spiralizer according to the manufacturer's directions.

4. Add your zoodles to the pot along with your chopped cilantro or parsley. Stir and remove the pot from the heat. The zoodles will cook quickly just from sitting in the hot soup. Taste and add extra salt and black pepper, if desired.

TIP

- You absolutely can use 20 ounces (560 g) of store-bought zoodles; however, they tend to be very thin and fall apart quickly. Spiralizing your own noodles means you can get them nice and thick so they hold up well in a soup.

- If you're planning to meal prep with this recipe, leave the zoodles out and incorporate them only when you're ready to eat. Reheated zoodles can get too soft because they contain so much water. Let everything else simmer (even the fresh herbs), freeze or refrigerate, and then add the zoodles when it's time to chow down!

healthy 30-minute hamburger soup

I feel like most people grew up eating hamburger soup, but for some reason, I didn't discover it until adulthood. And I do love it! My version is made with only wholesome ingredients and is ready in about 25 minutes. In order to cook your soup quickly and avoid it being too much like a stew, cut your potatoes and other veggies into ½-inch (1 cm) pieces. This means you'll also get a little of everything in every bite!

PREP TIME 10 minutes
TOTAL TIME 30 minutes
MAKES 8 to 10 servings

- 1 pound (455 g) 93% lean ground beef
- ½ white or yellow onion, diced into ½-inch (1 cm) pieces
- 1 tablespoon (10 g) minced garlic
- 32 ounces (946 ml) beef stock
- 2 medium white sweet potatoes, peeled and cut into 1-inch (2.5 cm) cubes (see Tip)
- 2 medium carrots, peeled and cut into half circles ¼ inch (6 mm) thick
- 1 cup (100 g) chopped green beans
- 1 can (14.5 ounces, or 410 g) diced tomatoes
- 2 tablespoons (32 g) tomato paste
- 1 teaspoon dried thyme
- 1 teaspoon dried oregano
- 1 teaspoon salt
- 1 teaspoon onion powder
- ½ teaspoon black pepper
- ¼ cup (15 g) chopped fresh parsley

1. Add the ground beef and onion to a soup pot over medium-high heat. Use a spatula to crumble your beef and sauté until browned, stirring occasionally, about 5 minutes. Add the garlic and sauté for another minute so the garlic is golden in color.

2. Add the stock, sweet potatoes, carrots, green beans, tomatoes, tomato paste, thyme, oregano, salt, onion powder, and black pepper. Cover, reduce the heat to medium, and simmer until the veggies are tender, 15 to 20 minutes. Taste and add extra salt or black pepper, if desired. Ladle into bowls and top with fresh chopped parsley.

TIP

- I'm using white sweet potatoes here because they have a drier texture than their orange counterparts, so they better resemble a russet. You can, of course, use any potato you like!

chicken & "rice" soup

There are so many flavorful aromatics and fresh herbs in this lovely soup! Plus, the chicken cooks in the broth to give you a robust flavor that soothes the soul and fills the belly.

PREP TIME 5 minutes
TOTAL TIME 30 minutes
MAKES 6 to 8 servings

1 tablespoon (15 ml) extra-virgin olive oil or avocado oil

1 white or yellow onion, diced into ½-inch (1 cm) pieces

3 ribs celery, diced into ½-inch (1 cm) pieces

8 ounces (225 g) mushrooms, chopped

2 teaspoons minced garlic

32 ounces (946 ml) chicken stock

1 pound (455 g) boneless, skinless chicken breasts, cut into 1-inch (2.5 cm) pieces

1½ teaspoons fresh chopped rosemary

1½ teaspoons chopped fresh dill

1½ teaspoons salt

½ teaspoon black pepper

2 cups (8 ounces, 225 g) fresh or frozen cauliflower rice

1. Add the oil to a soup pot over medium-high heat. Once hot, add the onion, celery, and mushrooms. Sauté until the onion and mushrooms are tender, about 5 minutes. Add the garlic and sauté for another minute so the garlic is golden in color.

2. Add the stock, chicken, rosemary, dill, salt, and black pepper. Bring to a boil over high heat. Cover, reduce the heat to medium, and simmer for 10 minutes.

3. Stir in the cauliflower rice. Cover and simmer until the cauliflower is soft and the chicken is cooked through, completely opaque and juices run clear, another 10 minutes. Taste and add more salt and pepper, if desired.

6

swoonworthy one-dish desserts

I never tire of breakfast food. How about you? In fact, I believe breakfast shouldn't be limited to that first meal of the day. I'll whip up a hash or frittata for lunch or dinner when the craving hits!

skillet blueberry almond cobbler

There's something about a cobbler with bubbling blueberries, orange, and almond. That flavor combo is divine, isn't it? Top it with coconut whipped cream for something special.

PREP TIME 10 minutes
TOTAL TIME 30 minutes + rest time
MAKES 8 servings

BLUEBERRY FILLING

4 cups (580 g) fresh blueberries

⅓ cup (115 g) raw honey

Zest of 1 orange

3 tablespoons (45 ml) fresh orange juice

2 teaspoons almond extract

⅛ teaspoon salt

CRUMBLE TOPPING

¾ cup (83 g) chopped pecans

¼ cup (28 g) almond flour

¼ cup (60 g) unsweetened applesauce

1 tablespoon (7 g) coconut flour

½ teaspoon almond extract

¼ teaspoon ground cinnamon

2 tablespoons (28 ml) unsweetened almond milk

1. Preheat the oven to 450°F (230°C, or gas mark 8).

2. Make the Blueberry Filling: In a 10-inch (25.5 cm) cast-iron skillet, gently combine the blueberries, honey, zest, orange juice, almond extract, and salt. Spread in an even layer.

3. Make the Crumble Topping: Iin a large bowl, stir together the pecans, almond flour, applesauce, coconut flour, almond extract, and cinnamon. The final texture should be soft and clumpy.

4. Use your hands to scatter the crumble topping on top of the blueberry mixture. Gently press the topping down into your blueberries. The topping shouldn't be submerged; we just don't want it sitting completely on top of the blueberries. As it cooks, some of it will work its way down into your fruit filling.

5. Bake for 10 minutes. Remove from the oven and reduce the temperature to 425°F (220°C, or gas mark 7).

6. Drizzle the almond milk on top of the crumble. Bake in the oven and bake until the topping has some nice browning and the blueberries are bubbly, another 7 to 8 minutes.

7. After baking, let the cobbler sit for 15 minutes to set up. Serve warm or at room temperature.

MAKE COCONUT WHIPPED CREAM

Chill one can of coconut cream or coconut milk in the fridge overnight. (I recommend using canned coconut cream because it has less water.) Once chilled, scoop out the thick cream that separates to the top of the can. (Leave the liquid in the can. We won't use it for this recipe!) Whip using a stand mixer or handheld mixer for 2 to 3 minutes until soft peaks form. If you prefer your whipped cream a little sweeter, you can add a dash of vanilla and/or your sweetener of choice.

chocolate mousse–stuffed strawberries

To create the chocolate mousse we're stuffing our strawberries with, refrigerate your coconut cream overnight. That will make it as firm as possible so that it doesn't become thin when blending. The finished mousse is lightly sweet and won't overpower your strawberries!

PREP TIME 20 minutes + overnight chill time
TOTAL TIME 20 minutes
MAKES 10 tO 12 servings

2 cans (13½ ounces, or 380 g, each) coconut cream (see Tip)

2 pounds (900 g) fresh large strawberries

2½ tablespoons (12.5 g) unsweetened cacao or cocoa powder

2 tablespoons (28 ml) pure maple syrup or (40 g) raw honey (For vegan dishes, use pure maple syrup.)

1. Chill the coconut cream in the refrigerator overnight. We're trying to encourage separation of the cream from the liquid.

2. Rinse the strawberries and pat dry. Remove the stems from the strawberries and then use a melon baller or small knife to scoop out a hole in the top of each.

3. If you want your strawberries to stand up, use a knife to cut a bit off the bottom of each strawberry so that it's flat and straight. Set aside while you make the chocolate mousse filling.

4. Carefully scoop out the solid coconut cream from the can and add it to a mixing bowl. Do not stir or shake the can. (Leave the liquid in the can for use in a smoothie or in a sauce later.)

5. Beat the hardened coconut cream with a mixer until creamy and smooth, 30 seconds. Check for lumps and make sure you smooth those out before moving to the next step. (Or just remove any stubborn clumps that refuse to cooperate.)

6. Add the cacao or cocoa powder and maple syrup or honey. Mix with a spatula or your beater until thoroughly combined.

7. To fill the strawberries, spoon the mousse into a resealable plastic bag with one corner cut off (or a piping bag if you're fancy). Pipe into each hollowed-out strawberry.

TIP

- Refrigerate any leftover mousse and use it as a fruit dip! It will continue to thicken in the fridge, so just give it a good stir before using.
- You can use coconut milk if you don't have coconut cream; however, you will not have as much solid cream in the can because the milk has a higher water content. This means you'll have less mousse. Start with 1½ tablespoons (25 ml) maple syrup and 1 tablespoon (5 g) cocoa powder

skillet apple cinnamon cobbler

This skillet cobbler is everything you'd want in an apple pie but much simpler to make and contains no refined sugar. I promise you, nobody will notice. Honey and applesauce make this dessert perfectly sweet! Top it with coconut whipped cream, if desired.

PREP TIME 10 minutes
TOTAL TIME 30 minutes + rest time
MAKES 8 servings

APPLE FILLING

6 cups (900 g) diced apples, ½-inch (1 cm) dice (unpeeled) (see Tip)

2 tablespoons (28 g) coconut oil

½ cup (170 g) raw honey

½ teaspoon ground cinnamon

¼ teaspoon ground nutmeg

CRUMBLE TOPPING

¾ cup (90 g) chopped walnuts, divided

¼ cup (28 g) almond flour

¼ cup (60 g) unsweetened applesauce

1 tablespoon (7 g) coconut flour

½ teaspoon vanilla extract

¼ teaspoon ground cinnamon

2 tablespoons (28 ml) unsweetened almond milk

1. Preheat the oven to 450°F (230°C, or gas mark 8).

2. Make the Apple Filling: Add the apples and oil to a 10-inch (25.5 cm) cast-iron skillet over medium-high heat. Sauté, stirring occasionally, until the apples are fairly soft, about 5 minutes. (To speed this up you can cover your skillet, but just be sure to uncover and let some of the excess liquid cook off before moving on to the next step.)

3. Meanwhile, make the Crumble Topping: In a large bowl, combine ½ cup (60 g) of the walnuts, almond flour, applesauce, coconut flour, vanilla, and cinnamon. The final texture should be clumpy.

4. Stir the honey, cinnamon, and nutmeg into the sautéed apples and remove from the heat.

5. Use your hands to scatter the crumble topping on top of the apple mixture. Gently press the topping down into your apples. The topping shouldn't be submerged in the filling; we just don't want it sitting completely on top of the apples. As it cooks, some of it will work its way down into your fruit filling.

6. Drizzle the almond milk over the topping and bake until bubbly and you have some browning on the crust, about 15 minutes.

7. Remove from the oven and sprinkle the remaining ¼ cup (30 g) walnuts on top. Let the cobbler sit for 15 minutes to set up. Serve warm or at room temperature.

TIP

- I recommend dicing your apples for this recipe, instead of using slices, as it speeds up the cooking process. And there's no need to peel those apples! The peel softens beautifully as it cooks.

dairy-free chocolate pudding

Oh, just wait until you try this decadent pudding! It is so sweet, creamy, and thick, it tastes like you're really indulging—but you can feel oh-so-good about these ingredients.

PREP TIME 5 minutes
TOTAL TIME 15 minutes + chill time
MAKES 4 servings

1 can (13½ ounces, or 380 g) coconut cream

½ cup (40 g) unsweetened cacao or cocoa powder

½ cup (120 ml) pure maple syrup or (170 g) raw honey (For vegan dishes, use pure maple syrup.)

½ teaspoon vanilla extract

3 tablespoons (27 g) arrowroot flour

3 tablespoons (45 ml) cold water

1. Add the coconut cream, cacao or cocoa powder, maple syrup or honey, and vanilla to a medium saucepan. Bring to a boil, whisking frequently. As soon as it begins to boil, remove from the heat.

2. Combine the arrowroot flour and water in a small jar. Shake until well combined. Pour the slurry into your warm pudding mixture, whisking so that the pudding is smooth and creamy. You'll notice the pudding has thickened but isn't quite as thick as you'll want it. Pour into a bowl, cover with plastic wrap, and place in the freezer for 1 hour to firm up.

TIP

- This pudding will keep in the refrigerator, covered, for up to 5 days, so it's ideal for meal prep!

sheet-pan blueberry granola

This Paleo granola is delicious for breakfast or snacking! It's loaded with nuts, pumpkin seeds, and dried blueberries. Plus, it's lightly sweetened with zero refined sugar. Bake and then store in an airtight container for up to 2 weeks of enjoyment.

PREP TIME 10 minutes
TOTAL TIME 30 minutes + cooling time
MAKES about 8 cups (25 servings, ⅓ cup [85 g] each)

2 cups (200 g) walnuts

2 cups (200 g) pecan halves

2 cups (220 g) slivered almonds

½ cup (70 g) pumpkin seeds

½ cup (120 ml) pure maple syrup or (170 g) raw honey (For vegan dishes, use pure maple syrup.)

3 tablespoons (45 g) coconut oil, melted

1 teaspoon ground cinnamon

2 cups (240 g) dried blueberries

1. Preheat the oven to 325°F (170°C, or gas mark 3) and set the oven rack to the middle position. Line a 12 x 17-inch (30 x 43 cm) baking sheet with parchment paper.

2. Coarsely chop the walnuts and pecans. You don't want them to be super small, but you don't want to have any giant pieces in there either. Spread in a single layer on the prepared baking sheet.

3. Scatter the almonds and pumpkin seeds on top.

4. In a small bowl, stir together the maple syrup or honey, oil, and cinnamon. Pour over your nut mixture and then use a spatula to stir it all together. You want everything thoroughly coated. Spread everything into an even layer.

5. Bake for 18 minutes and then turn the broiler to high. Broil (on the same middle baking rack) for 1½ to 2 minutes to achieve a light golden color. Watch your granola as it broils because it can quickly burn.

6. Remove from the oven and stir in the dried blueberries. Spread everything back into an even layer and let cool completely. The granola will get crispy as it cools.

7. Once completely cooled, store in an airtight container at room temperature. It will be good for at least 2 weeks, but I bet you'll have it all gobbled up long before then!

TIP

- Don't skimp on these blueberries! Make sure you select an unsweetened brand and use the full 2 cups (240 g). It's worth it because they really do add the perfect sweetness to each bite!

no-fuss fudgy brownies

So fudgy, dense, and perfectly soft, these brownies are made with Paleo baking flour, which is a premade blend of almond flour, coconut flour, and starches. For sweetness (because these are definitely sweet), we use coconut sugar and maple syrup. Want more good news? You don't need to break out your stand mixer. This dessert really is easy!

PREP TIME 5 minutes
TOTAL TIME 25 minutes + cooling time
MAKES 9 servings

1 cup (144 g) coconut sugar

½ cup (120 ml) pure maple syrup

¼ cup (56 g) coconut oil, melted

¼ cup (56 g) ghee, melted

2 large eggs

1½ teaspoons vanilla extract

¾ cups (69 g) Paleo baking flour

¼ cup (20 g) unsweetened cacao or cocoa powder

1. Preheat the oven to 400°F (200°C, or gas mark 6). Line a 9 x 9-inch (23 x 23 cm) baking pan with parchment paper.

2. In a large bowl, stir together the coconut sugar, maple syrup, oil, and ghee until well combined.

3. Add the eggs and vanilla. Stir well.

4. Stir in the Paleo baking flour and cacao powder until well combined. Transfer the batter to the prepared pan.

5. Bake for 17 to 20 minutes or until a toothpick inserted into the center of the brownies comes out with crumbs. The toothpick should not be clean but it shouldn't be completely wet either. (You're going to be on the lower side of that time if using metal and on the higher side of that time if using glass or ceramic.)

6. After baking, cool until set, about 15 minutes, on the counter or a wire rack. Remove the brownies from the pan by lifting the edges of the parchment paper and slice into 9 squares.

TIP

- As a general rule, light-colored metal pans are favored for brownies because they cook evenly and prevent overbrowning. You can (and I have) use glass or ceramic, but be aware that this type of cooking vessel means your batter may need to cook a bit longer. Since it takes longer for the center to cook, it's also easier to burn the edge pieces, so keep a close eye on it.

easy fruit bake

Is this easy fruit bake a dessert or a beautiful addition to a brunch? It's both! You can even use it as a topping for biscuits, pancakes, or waffles! It's just so versatile and yummy.

PREP TIME 10 minutes
TOTAL TIME 30 minutes
MAKES 8 servings

32 ounces (900 kg) frozen peach slices (see Tip)

2 cans (15 ounces, or 425 g, each) pear halves in 100% juice, drained (see Tip)

2 tablespoons (28 g) ghee, melted

1 teaspoon ground cinnamon

1 cup (100 g) fresh cranberries

⅓ cup (80 ml) pure maple syrup

1. Preheat the oven to 425°F (220°C, or gas mark 7).

2. Spread the frozen peaches in an even layer on the bottom of a 9 x 13-inch (23 x 33 cm) baking dish.

3. Add the pears on top of your peaches. Do not use the juice as this will give you too much liquid. (Why not incorporate that sweet juice in a smoothie instead? There's no sense wasting it!)

4. In a small bowl, combine the ghee and cinnamon. Pour over the peaches and pears.

5. Spread the cranberries on top and then drizzle the maple syrup over all the fruit.

6. Bake until the cranberries are bursting and the peaches have softened, about 20 minutes.

TIP

- Using canned pears and frozen peaches drastically cuts both our prep time (no chopping anything!) and baking time, so we can serve up this roasted fruit quickly. You can certainly use fresh fruit, if you prefer, but increase the baking time to somewhere closer to 45 minutes in order to give the fruit enough time to fully soften.

easy paleo chocolate muffins

These muffins are chocolaty and soft but made with simple Paleo ingredients! Cacao powder and your favorite dark chocolate bar work together to give us the rich flavor we crave in chocolate desserts. Plus, these muffins are incredibly easy to make. You can get the batter ready for the oven in as little as 5 minutes! How about that for a good-for-you sweet treat you can enjoy whenever the mood strikes?

PREP TIME 5 minutes
TOTAL TIME 25 minutes + rest time
MAKES 12 muffins

1 cup (112 g) almond flour

¼ cup (28 g) coconut flour

¼ cup (20 g) unsweetened cacao or cocoa powder

½ cup (72 g) coconut sugar

1 teaspoon baking soda

3 large eggs

1 cup (235 ml) almond milk

¼ cup (56 g) coconut oil, melted

1½ teaspoons vanilla extract

2½ ounces (70 g) Paleo dark chocolate bar, finely chopped (see Tip)

1. Preheat the oven to 375°F (190°C, or gas mark 5). Line a 12-cup muffin pan with liners.

2. In a large bowl, stir together the almond flour, coconut flour, cacao powder, coconut sugar, and baking soda until well combined.

3. Add the eggs, almond milk, oil, and vanilla. Stir well.

4. Fold in the chopped chocolate bar pieces.

5. Spoon the batter into the prepared muffin pan, dividing the batter evenly and filling each liner three-fourths of the way full.

6. Bake until a toothpick inserted into the center of the muffins comes out with crumbs, about 20 minutes. The toothpick should not be clean, but it shouldn't be completely wet either.

7. After baking, let the cupcakes cool briefly before enjoying.

TIP

- You're welcome to use your favorite Paleo chocolate bar in this recipe. The one I often select is 72% cacao and includes only cacao, coconut sugar, and cacao butter.